LIFE
Lessons
WITH MAX LUCADO

W9-BID-891

BOOK OF JOHN

WHEN GOD BECAME MAN

MAX LUCADO

Prepared by

THE LIVINGSTONE CORPORATION

THOMAS NELSON
Since 1798

NASHVILLE   DALLAS   MEXICO CITY   RIO DE JANEIRO

Life Lessons with Max Lucado—Book of John

© 2006, Thomas Nelson, Inc.

Published in Nashville, Tennessee, by Thomas Nelson. Thomas Nelson is a registered trademark of Thomas Nelson, Inc.

Produced with the assistance of the Livingstone Corporation (www.livingstonecorp.com). Project staff include Jake Barton, Joel Bartlett, Andy Culbertson, Mary Horner Collins, and Will Reaves.

Editor: Neil Wilson

Scripture quotations marked "NCV™" are taken from the New Century Version®. © 2005 by Thomas Nelson, Inc. Used by permission. All rights reserved.

Scripture quotations marked "NKJV™" are taken from the New King James Version®. © 1982 by Thomas Nelson, Inc. Used by permission. All rights reserved.

Scriptures quotations marked (NLT) are taken from the Holy Bible, New Living Translation, © 1996. Used by permission of Tyndale House Publishers, Inc, Wheaton, Illinois 60189. All rights reserved.

Material for the "Inspiration" sections taken from the following books:

The Applause of Heaven. © 1990, 1996, 1999 by Max Lucado. W Publishing Group, a Division of Thomas Nelson, Inc., Nashville, Tennessee.

God Came Near. © 2004 by Max Lucado. W Publishing Group, a Division of Thomas Nelson, Inc., Nashville, Tennessee.

He Still Moves Stones. © 1993 by Max Lucado. W Publishing Group, a Division of Thomas Nelson, Inc., Nashville, Tennessee.

In the Eye of the Storm. © 1991 by Max Lucado. W Publishing Group, a Division of Thomas Nelson, Inc., Nashville, Tennessee.

Just Like Jesus. © 2003 by Max Lucado. W Publishing Group, a Division of Thomas Nelson, Inc., Nashville, Tennessee.

Next Door Savior. © 2003 by Max Lucado. W Publishing Group, a Division of Thomas Nelson, Inc., Nashville, Tennessee.

Six Hours One Friday. © 2004 by Max Lucado. W Publishing Group, a Division of Thomas Nelson, Inc., Nashville, Tennessee.

When God Whispers Your Name. © 1994, 1999 by Max Lucado. W Publishing Group, a Division of Thomas Nelson, Inc., Nashville, Tennessee.

Cover Art and Interior Design by Kirk Luttrell of the Livingstone Corporation

Interior Composition by Rachel Hawkins of the Livingstone Corporation

ISBN: 978-1-4185-0944-6

Printed in the United States of America.

10 11 12 13 14 WC 19 18 17 16 15

LIFE Lessons

WITH MAX LUCADO

CONTENTS

HOW TO STUDY THE BIBLE

This is a peculiar book you are holding. Words crafted in another language. Deeds done in a distant era. Events recorded in a far-off land. Counsel offered to a foreign people. This is a peculiar book.

It's surprising that anyone reads it. It's too old. Some of its writings date back five thousand years. It's too bizarre. The book speaks of incredible floods, fires, earthquakes, and people with supernatural abilities. It's too radical. The Bible calls for undying devotion to a carpenter who called himself God's Son.

Logic says this book shouldn't survive. Too old, too bizarre, too radical.

The Bible has been banned, burned, scoffed, and ridiculed. Scholars have mocked it as foolish. Kings have branded it as illegal. A thousand times over the grave has been dug and the dirge has begun, but somehow the Bible never stays in the grave. Not only has it survived, it has thrived. It is the single most popular book in all of history. It has been the best-selling book in the world for years!

There is no way on earth to explain it. Which perhaps is the only explanation. The answer? The Bible's durability is not found on earth; it is found in heaven. For the millions who have tested its claims and claimed its promises, there is but one answer: the Bible is God's book and God's voice.

As you read it, you would be wise to give some thought to two questions. What is the purpose of the Bible? and How do I study the Bible? Time spent reflecting on these two issues will greatly enhance your Bible study.

What is the purpose of the Bible? Let the Bible itself answer that question.

Since you were a child you have known the Holy Scriptures which are able to make you wise. And that wisdom leads to salvation through faith in Christ Jesus. (2 Tim. 3:15 NCV)

The purpose of the Bible? Salvation. God's highest passion is to get his children home. His book, the Bible, describes his plan of salvation. The purpose of the Bible is to proclaim God's plan and passion to save his children.

That is the reason this book has endured through the centuries. It dares to tackle the toughest questions about life: Where do I go after I die? Is there a God? What do I do with my fears? The Bible offers answers to these crucial questions. It is the treasure map that leads us to God's highest treasure—eternal life.

But how do we use the Bible? Countless copies of Scripture sit unread on bookshelves and nightstands simply because people don't know how to read it. What can we do to make the Bible real in our lives? The clearest answer is found in the words of Jesus. He promised:

Ask, and God will give to you. Search, and you will find. Knock, and the door will open for you. (Matt. 7:7 NCV)

The first step in understanding the Bible is asking God to help us. We should read prayerfully. If anyone understands God's Word, it is because of God and not the reader.

But the Helper will teach you everything and will cause you to remember all that I told you. The Helper is the Holy Spirit whom the Father will send in my name. (John 14:26 NCV)

Before reading the Bible, pray. Invite God to speak to you. Don't go to Scripture looking for your idea; go searching for his.

Not only should we read the Bible prayerfully, we should read it carefully. *Search and you will find* is the pledge. The Bible is not a newspaper to be skimmed but rather a mine to be quarried.

Search for it like silver, and hunt for it like hidden treasure. Then you will understand respect for the Lord, and you will find that you know God. (Prov. 2:4–5 NCV)

Any worthy find requires effort. The Bible is no exception. To understand the Bible you don't have to be brilliant, but you must be willing to roll up your sleeves and search.

Be a worker who is not ashamed and who uses the true teaching in the right way. (2 Tim. 2:15 NCV)

Here's a practical point. Study the Bible a bit at a time. Hunger is not satisfied by eating twenty-one meals in one sitting once a week. The body needs a steady diet to remain strong. So does the soul. When God sent food to his people in the wilderness, he didn't provide loaves already made. Instead, he sent them manna in the shape of *"thin flakes like frost . . . on the desert ground"* (Ex. 16:14 NCV).

God gave manna in limited portions. God sends spiritual food the same way. He opens the heavens with just enough nutrients for today's hunger. He provides *"a command here, a command there. A rule here, a rule there. A little lesson here, a little lesson there"* (Isa. 28:10 NCV).

Don't be discouraged if your reading reaps a small harvest. Some days a lesser portion is all that is needed. What is important is to search every day for that day's message. A steady diet of God's Word over a lifetime builds a healthy soul and mind.

A little girl returned from her first day at school. Her mom asked, "Did you learn anything?"

"Apparently not enough," the girl responded, "I have to go back tomorrow and the next day and the next . . ." Such is the case with learning. And such is the case with Bible study. Understanding comes little by little over a lifetime.

There is a third step in understanding the Bible. After the asking and seeking comes the knocking. After you ask and search, then knock.

Knock, and the door will open for you. (Matt. 7:7 NCV)

To knock is to stand at God's door. To make yourself available. To climb the steps, cross the porch, stand at the doorway, and volunteer. Knocking goes beyond the realm of thinking and into the realm of acting.

To knock is to ask, What can I do? How can I obey? Where can I go?

It's one thing to know what to do. It's another to do it. But for those who do it, those who choose to obey, a special reward awaits them.

The truly happy are those who carefully study God's perfect law that makes people free, and they continue to study it. They do not forget what they heard, but they obey what God's teaching says. Those who do this will be made happy. (James 1:25 NCV)

What a promise. Happiness comes to those who do what they read! It's the same with medicine. If you only read the label but ignore the pills, it won't help. It's the same with food. If you only read the recipe but never cook, you won't be fed. And it's the same with the Bible. If you only read the words but never obey, you'll never know the joy God has promised.

Ask. Search. Knock. Simple, isn't it? Why don't you give it a try? If you do, you'll see why you are holding the most remarkable book in history.

INTRODUCTION TO THE BOOK OF JOHN

He's an old man, this one who sits on the stool and leans against the wall. Eyes closed and face soft, were it not for his hand stroking his beard, you'd think he was asleep.

Some in the room assume he is. He does this often during worship. As the people sing, his eyes will close and his chin will fall until it rests on his chest, and there he will remain motionless. Silent.

Those who know him well know better. They know he is not resting. He is traveling. Atop the music he journeys back, back, back until he is young again. Strong again. There again. There on the seashore with James and the apostles. There on the trail with the disciples and the women. There in the temple with Caiaphas and the accusers.

It's been sixty years, but John sees him still. The decades took John's strength, but they didn't take his memory. The years dulled his sight, but they didn't dull his vision. The seasons may have wrinkled his face, but they didn't soften his love.

He had been with God. God had been with him. How could he forget?

The wine that moments before had been water—John could still taste it.

The mud placed on the eyes of the blind man in Jerusalem—John could still remember it.

The aroma of Mary's perfume as it filled the room—John could still smell it.

And the voice. Oh, the voice. His voice. John could still hear it.

I am the light of the world . . . I am the door . . . I am the way, the truth, the life.

I will come back and take you to be with me.

Those who believe in me will have life even if they die.

John could hear him. John could see him. Scenes branded on his heart. Words seared into his soul. John would never forget. How could he? He had been there.

He opens his eyes and blinks. The singing has stopped. The teaching has begun. John looks at the listeners and listens to the teacher.

If only you could have been there, he thinks.

But most of the people here weren't even born then. And most who were with Jesus are dead. Peter is gone. So is James. Nathaniel, Martha, Bartholomew. They are all gone. Even Paul, the apostle who came late, is dead.

Only John remains.

He looks again at the church. Small but earnest. They lean forward to hear the teacher. John listens to him. What a task. Speaking of one he never saw. Explaining words he never heard. John is there if the teacher needs him.

But what will happen when John is gone? What will the teacher do then? When John's voice is silent and his tongue stilled? Who will tell them how Jesus silenced the waves? Will they hear how he fed the thousands? Will they remember how he prayed for unity?

How will they know? If only they could have been there.

Suddenly, in his heart he knows what to do.

Later, under the light of a sunlit shaft, the old fisherman unfolds the scroll and begins to write the story of his life . . .

In the beginning was the Word . . .

LESSON ONE

WHEN GOD BECAME MAN

MAX
LUCADO

REFLECTION

Christ was born on earth by the will of God. When we accept him as Savior, we, too, are born (for a second time) through the will of God. We become "children of God." This is our second birth, our spiritual birth into eternal life. Describe some of the events surrounding your "second birth."

SITUATION

The language and tone of John's writing may be quite different from the other three Gospels, but the subject is clearly the same—Jesus Christ. The first three words of this book echo the first verse of the Bible, "In the beginning . . ." (Gen. 1:1, NKJV). The Gospels of Matthew and Luke highlight Jesus' human lineage; John highlights his divine nature. From the very first verse, John sets Jesus in the center of God's eternal plan.

OBSERVATION

Read John 1:1–18 from the NCV or the NKJV.

NCV

¹*In the beginning there was the Word. The Word was with God, and the Word was God.* ²*He was with God in the beginning.* ³*All things were made by him, and nothing was made without him.* ⁴*In him there was life, and that life was the light of all people.* ⁵*The Light shines in the darkness, and the darkness has not overpowered it.*

⁶*There was a man named John who was sent by God.* ⁷*He came to tell people the truth about the Light so that through him all people could hear about the Light and believe.* ⁸*John was not the Light, but he came to tell people the truth about the Light.* ⁹*The true Light that gives light to all was coming into the world!*

¹⁰*The Word was in the world, and the world was made by him, but the world did not know him.* ¹¹*He came to the world that was his own, but his own people did not accept him.* ¹²*But to all who did accept him and believe in him he gave the right to become children of God.* ¹³*They did not become his children in any human way—by any human parents or human desire. They were born of God.*

¹⁴*The Word became a human and lived among us. We saw his glory—the glory that belongs to the only Son of the Father—and he was full of grace and truth.* ¹⁵*John tells the truth about him and cries out, saying, "This is the One I told you about: 'The One who comes after me is greater than I am, because he was living before me.'"*

¹⁶*Because he was full of grace and truth, from him we all received one gift after another.* ¹⁷*The law was given through Moses, but grace and truth came through Jesus Christ.* ¹⁸*No one has ever seen God. But God the only Son is very close to the Father, and he has shown us what God is like.*

NKJV

¹*In the beginning was the Word, and the Word was with God, and the Word was God.* ²*He was in the beginning with God.* ³*All things were made through Him, and without Him nothing was made that was made.* ⁴*In Him was life, and the life was the light of men.* ⁵*And the light shines in the darkness, and the darkness did not comprehend it.*

⁶*There was a man sent from God, whose name was John.* ⁷*This man came for a witness, to bear witness of the Light, that all through him might believe.* ⁸*He was not that Light, but was sent to bear witness of that Light.* ⁹*That was the true Light which gives light to every man coming into the world.*

¹⁰*He was in the world, and the world was made through Him, and the world did not know Him.* ¹¹*He came to His own, and His own did not receive Him.* ¹²*But as many as received Him, to them He gave the right to become children of God, to those who believe in His name:* ¹³*who were born, not of blood, nor of the will of the flesh, nor of the will of man, but of God.*

14And the Word became flesh and dwelt among us, and we beheld His glory, the glory as of the only begotten of the Father, full of grace and truth.

15John bore witness of Him and cried out, saying, "This was He of whom I said, 'He who comes after me is preferred before me, for He was before me.'"

16And of His fullness we have all received, and grace for grace. 17For the law was given through Moses, but grace and truth came through Jesus Christ.

18No one has seen God at any time. The only begotten Son, who is in the bosom of the Father, He has declared Him.

EXPLORATION

1. What evidences stand out for you, indicating that Jesus' birth and life were unique? (For background, you may want to review some of the prophecies about the Messiah. Jesus' birth and life fulfilled all Old Testament prophecies regarding the Messiah. Micah 5:2 is fulfilled in Matthew 2:1–6; Isaiah 7:14 is fulfilled in Luke 1:26–38; Psalm 22:14–17 is fulfilled in Mark 15:20, 25; and Isaiah 53:5–12 is fulfilled in John 1:29; 11:49–52.)

2. What does this passage reveal about Jesus' mission?

3. What does Jesus' life as a man tell us about God as Father?

4. Jesus brought grace and truth to us. How does this benefit your life?

5. Many people did not believe that Jesus was God's Son. What did they miss by not receiving him?

INSPIRATION

It all happened in a moment, a most remarkable moment.

As moments go, that one appeared no different than any other. If you could somehow pick it up off the timeline and examine it, it would look exactly like the ones that have passed while you have read these words. It came and it went. It was preceded and succeeded by others just like it. It was one of the countless moments that have marked time since eternity became measurable.

But in reality, that particular moment was like none other. For through that segment of time a spectacular thing occurred. God became a man. While the creatures of earth walked unaware, Divinity arrived. Heaven opened herself and placed her most precious one in a human womb.

The omnipotent, in one instant, made himself breakable. He who had been spirit became pierceable. He who was larger than the universe became an embryo. And he who sustains the world with a word chose to be dependent upon the nourishment of a young girl.

God as a fetus. Holiness sleeping in a womb. The creator of life being created.

God was given eyebrows, elbows, two kidneys, and a spleen. He stretched against the walls and floated in the amniotic fluids of his mother.

God had come near.

He came, not as a flash of light or as an unapproachable conqueror, but as one whose first cries were heard by a peasant girl and a sleepy carpenter. The hands that first held him were unmanicured, calloused, and dirty.

No silk. No ivory. No hype. No party. No hoopla.

Were it not for the shepherds, there would have been no reception. And were it not for a group of star-gazers, there would have been no gifts.

Angels watched as Mary changed God's diaper. The universe watched with wonder as The Almighty learned to walk. Children played in the street with him. And had the synagogue leader in Nazareth known who was listening to his sermons . . .

For thirty-three years he would feel everything you and I have ever felt. He felt weak. He grew weary. He was afraid of failure. He was susceptible to wooing women. He got colds, burped, and had body odor. His feelings got hurt. His feet got tired. And his head ached.

To think of Jesus in such a light is—well, it seems almost irreverent, doesn't it? It's not something we like to do; it's uncomfortable. It is much easier to keep the humanity out of the incarnation. Clean the manure from around the manger. Wipe the sweat out of his eyes. Pretend he never snored or blew his nose or hit his thumb with a hammer.

He's easier to stomach that way. There is something about keeping him divine that keeps him distant, packaged, predictable.

But don't do it. For heaven's sake, don't. Let him be as human as he intended to be. Let him into the mire and muck of our world. For only if we let him in can he pull us out. (From *God Came Near* by Max Lucado)

REACTION

6. What surprises you about Jesus coming to earth as a human being? (You may have questions about the mystery of the Incarnation. The following passages offer some insight: Matthew 16:27; John 1:14; 10:37–38; 14:7–13; 17:22; Colossians 2:9; Hebrews 1:1–3.)

7. What is comforting or encouraging about God taking on a human form?

8. In what way does this truth inspire you?

9. What does Jesus' willingness to become a human being reveal about his heart?

10. In what ways would your life be different if Jesus had not yet come to earth?

11. How can I be a witness to others of the light of Christ?

LIFE LESSONS

John introduces his Gospel as the ultimate life lesson. One of Jesus' attributes that he highlights is the fact that Jesus is *life*. He offers true life. He offers eternal life. As you will discover throughout these lessons, the prologue of John acts like an overture in a symphony. The themes you've just begun to think about will be examined repeatedly in the lessons to come. This study is an opportunity to know life as you've never known him before.

DEVOTION

Blessed Lord and God, we come to you, thankful that you have pierced our world. You became flesh and dwelled among us. You saw us in our fallen state, and you reached in and pulled us out. You offered us salvation; you offered us mercy. We thank you for what you have done for us.

For more Bible passages about God becoming a man, see John 14:6–7; 1 Corinthians 8:5–6; Galatians 4:4; Philippians 2:7–8; Colossians 1:15–20; 1 Timothy 3:16; Hebrews 2:14; 1 John 1:1–2; 4:2.

To complete the book of John during this twelve-part study, read John 1:1–34.

JOURNALING

How does the Light of God shine in my life each day?

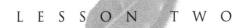

L E S S O N   T W O

A WEDDING
IN CANA

MAX
LUCADO

REFLECTION

Christian weddings often include references to Jesus' first miracle at a wedding. The fact that Jesus showed up for the occasion makes it a significant event. We hope Jesus is still showing up for weddings. Think of the most memorable wedding you have attended. What made it so memorable?

SITUATION

Weddings in Jesus' day were extended community events. They often lasted a week or more. Hospitality ruled the day, and families were under significant social pressure to provide lavishly for their guests. The problem that arose because the wine ran out created a major crisis. Mary tried to help and enlisted her son's assistance in finding a solution. Even she probably didn't expect the results that followed.

OBSERVATION

Read John 2:1–11 from the NCV or the NKJV.

NCV

1Two days later there was a wedding in the town of Cana in Galilee. Jesus' mother was there, 2and Jesus and his followers were also invited to the wedding. 3When all the wine was gone, Jesus' mother said to him, "They have no more wine."

4Jesus answered, "Dear woman, why come to me? My time has not yet come."

5His mother said to the servants, "Do whatever he tells you to do."

6In that place there were six stone water jars that the Jews used in their washing ceremony. Each jar held about twenty or thirty gallons.

7Jesus said to the servants, "Fill the jars with water." So they filled the jars to the top.

8Then he said to them, "Now take some out and give it to the master of the feast."

So they took the water to the master. 9When he tasted it, the water had become wine. He did not know where the wine came from, but the servants who had brought the water knew. The master of the wedding called the bridegroom 10and said to him, "People always serve the best wine first. Later, after the guests have been drinking awhile, they serve the cheaper wine. But you have saved the best wine till now."

11So in Cana of Galilee Jesus did his first miracle. There he showed his glory, and his followers believed in him.

NKJV

1On the third day there was a wedding in Cana of Galilee, and the mother of Jesus was there. 2Now both Jesus and His disciples were invited to the wedding. 3And when they ran out of wine, the mother of Jesus said to Him, "They have no wine."

4Jesus said to her, "Woman, what does your concern have to do with Me? My hour has not yet come."

5His mother said to the servants, "Whatever He says to you, do it."

6Now there were set there six waterpots of stone, according to the manner of purification of the Jews, containing twenty or thirty gallons apiece. 7Jesus said to them, "Fill the waterpots with water." And they filled them up to the brim. 8And He said to them, "Draw some out now, and take it to the master of the feast." And they took it. 9When the master of the feast had tasted the water that was made wine, and did not know where it came from (but the servants who had drawn the water knew), the master of the feast called the bridegroom. 10And he said to him, "Every man at the beginning sets out the good wine, and when the guests have well drunk, then the inferior. You have kept the good wine until now!"

11This beginning of signs Jesus did in Cana of Galilee, and manifested His glory; and His disciples believed in Him.

EXPLORATION

1. Does it seem unusual to you that Jesus would attend a wedding? Why or why not?

2. Why do you think Jesus chose to attend this wedding?

3. For whose benefit did Jesus do this miracle? (The immediate answer may seem obvious, but consider verse 11.)

4. What characteristic of Jesus did this miracle reveal?

5. How did this miracle affect the lives of the people around Jesus?

INSPIRATION

Picture six men walking on a narrow road . . . The men's faces are eager, but common. Their leader is confident, but unknown. They call him Rabbi; he looks more like a laborer. And well he should, for he's spent far more time building than teaching. But this week the teaching has begun.

Where are they going? To the temple to worship? To the synagogue to teach? To the hills to pray? They haven't been told, but they each have their own idea . . .

Maybe it was Andrew who asked it, "So Rabbi, where are you taking us? To the desert?"

"No," opines another, "he's taking us to the temple." . . .

Then a chorus of confusion breaks out and ends only when Jesus lifts his hand and says softly, "We're on our way to a wedding." . . .

"Why would we go to a wedding?"

Good question. Why would Jesus, on his first journey, take his followers to a party? Didn't they have work to do? Didn't he have principles to teach? Wasn't his time limited? How could a wedding fit with his purpose on earth?

Why did Jesus go to the wedding?

The answer? It's found in the second verse of John 2. "Jesus and his followers were also invited to the wedding." . . .

Big deal? I think so. I think it's significant that common folk in a little town enjoyed being with Jesus. I think it's noteworthy that the Almighty didn't act high and mighty. The Holy One wasn't holier-than-thou. The One who knew it all wasn't a know-it-all. The One who made the stars didn't keep his head in them. The One who owns all the stuff of earth never strutted it . . .

Jesus was a likable fellow. And his disciples should be the same. I'm not talking debauchery, drunkenness, and adultery. I'm not endorsing compromise, coarseness, or obscenity. I am simply crusading for the freedom to enjoy a good joke, enliven a dull party, and appreciate a fun evening . . .

We used to be good at it. What has happened to us? What happened to clean joy and loud laughter? Is it our neckties that choke us? Is it our diplomas that dignify us? Is it the pew that stiffens us? . . . I must confess: it's been awhile since I've been accused of having too much fun. How about you? (From *When God Whispers Your Name* by Max Lucado)

REACTION

6. Have you ever seen God provide in a miraculous way? Explain.

7. What prevents us from acknowledging God's provisions? If it's not a miracle, does it still come from God?

8. List some ways God has met your needs. How does remembering God's provision in the past encourage you to trust him with your present needs?

9. What simple pleasures bring you a sense of joy or fulfillment?

10. What sometimes holds you back from enjoying life? Why?

11. How do you think your Christian witness is affected when you don't take time to enjoy life?

LIFE LESSONS

What better way to start our examination of the Son of God than to witness his participation in the highs and lows of daily living? Before we give real attention to the ways Jesus wants to transform our lives, we must reach a better under-standing of his complete familiarity with our lives. He's comfortable with us. He knows us intimately—even those things no one else knows. When we come to him with our needs, when we realize that we can bring our emptiness to him, we're finally in a place where we can see his power at work in us.

DEVOTION

Lord Jesus, teach us to appreciate the simple pleasures in life and to enjoy the company of other people. May you walk with us, sharing life's pure pleasures and letting your light fall on life's common way.

For more Bible passages on enjoying life, see Deuteronomy 6:1–2; Psalm 91:15–16; Ecclesiastes 2:24–26; 3:22; 11:8–10; Romans 15:13; Ephesians 6:1–3; 1 Timothy 6:17.

To complete the book of John during this twelve-part study, read John 1:35–2:25.

JOURNALING

What reasons do I have to celebrate?

LESSON THREE

THE WOMAN
AT THE WELL

MAX
LUCADO

REFLECTION

Some of us can hardly remember a time when we weren't Christians. Others have become followers of Jesus more recently. Think about (and share with your group) the story of your conversion. How did your life change when you accepted Christ as your Savior?

SITUATION

The shortest route between Jerusalem in the south and Galilee in the north required walking through Samaria. For Jews in Jesus' day, this region was definitely on the "wrong side of the tracks." Samaritans were despised by Jews and did their best to return the compliment. Jesus seemed to go out of his way to challenge these traditional animosities. He showed up at the well of Sychar just as a woman arrived.

OBSERVATION

Read John 4:5–30 from the NCV or the NKJV.

NCV

⁵*In Samaria Jesus came to the town called Sychar, which is near the field Jacob gave to his son Joseph.* ⁶*Jacob's well was there. Jesus was tired from his long trip, so he sat down beside the well. It was about twelve o'clock noon.* ⁷*When a Samaritan woman came to the well to get some water, Jesus said to her, "Please give me a drink."* ⁸*(This happened while Jesus' followers were in town buying some food.)*

⁹*The woman said, "I am surprised that you ask me for a drink, since you are a Jewish man and I am a Samaritan woman." (Jewish people are not friends with Samaritans.)*

¹⁰*Jesus said, "If you only knew the free gift of God and who it is that is asking you for water, you would have asked him, and he would have given you living water."*

¹¹*The woman said, "Sir, where will you get this living water? The well is very deep, and you have nothing to get water with.* ¹²*Are you greater than Jacob, our father, who gave us this well and drank from it himself along with his sons and flocks?"*

13Jesus answered, "Everyone who drinks this water will be thirsty again, 14but whoever drinks the water I give will never be thirsty. The water I give will become a spring of water gushing up inside that person, giving eternal life."

15The woman said to him, "Sir, give me this water so I will never be thirsty again and will not have to come back here to get more water."

16Jesus told her, "Go get your husband and come back here."

17The woman answered, "I have no husband."

Jesus said to her, "You are right to say you have no husband. 18Really you have had five husbands, and the man you live with now is not your husband. You told the truth."

19The woman said, "Sir, I can see that you are a prophet. 20Our ancestors worshiped on this mountain, but you Jews say that Jerusalem is the place where people must worship."

21Jesus said, "Believe me, woman. The time is coming when neither in Jerusalem nor on this mountain will you actually worship the Father. 22You Samaritans worship something you don't understand. We understand what we worship, because salvation comes from the Jews. 23The time is coming when the true worshipers will worship the Father in spirit and truth, and that time is here already. You see, the Father too is actively seeking such people to worship him. 24God is spirit, and those who worship him must worship in spirit and truth."

25The woman said, "I know that the Messiah is coming." (Messiah is the One called Christ.) "When the Messiah comes, he will explain everything to us."

26Then Jesus said, "I am he—I, the one talking to you."

27Just then his followers came back from town and were surprised to see him talking with a woman. But none of them asked, "What do you want?" or "Why are you talking with her?"

28Then the woman left her water jar and went back to town. She said to the people, 29"Come and see a man who told me everything I ever did. Do you think he might be the Christ?" 30So the people left the town and went to see Jesus.

NKJV

5So He came to a city of Samaria which is called Sychar, near the plot of ground that Jacob gave to his son Joseph. 6Now Jacob's well was there. Jesus therefore, being wearied from His journey, sat thus by the well. It was about the sixth hour.

7A woman of Samaria came to draw water. Jesus said to her, "Give Me a drink." 8For His disciples had gone away into the city to buy food.

9Then the woman of Samaria said to Him, "How is it that You, being a Jew, ask a drink from me, a Samaritan woman?" For Jews have no dealings with Samaritans.

10Jesus answered and said to her, "If you knew the gift of God, and who it is who says to you, 'Give Me a drink,' you would have asked Him, and He would have given you living water."

11The woman said to Him, "Sir, You have nothing to draw with, and the well is deep. Where then do You get that living water? 12Are You greater than our father Jacob, who gave us the well, and drank from it himself, as well as his sons and his livestock?"

¹³Jesus answered and said to her, "Whoever drinks of this water will thirst again, ¹⁴but whoever drinks of the water that I shall give him will never thirst. But the water that I shall give him will become in him a fountain of water springing up into everlasting life."

¹⁵The woman said to Him, "Sir, give me this water, that I may not thirst, nor come here to draw."

¹⁶Jesus said to her, "Go, call your husband, and come here."

¹⁷The woman answered and said, "I have no husband."

Jesus said to her, "You have well said, 'I have no husband,' ¹⁸for you have had five hus- bands, and the one whom you now have is not your husband; in that you spoke truly." ¹⁹The woman said to Him, "Sir, I perceive that You are a prophet. ²⁰Our fathers worshiped on this mountain, and you Jews say that in Jerusalem is the place where one ought to worship."

²¹Jesus said to her, "Woman, believe Me, the hour is coming when you will neither on this mountain, nor in Jerusalem, worship the Father. ²²You worship what you do not know; we know what we worship, for salvation is of the Jews. ²³But the hour is coming, and now is, when the true worshipers will worship the Father in spirit and truth; for the Father is seeking such to worship Him. ²⁴God is Spirit, and those who worship Him must worship in spirit and truth."

²⁵The woman said to Him, "I know that Messiah is coming" (who is called Christ). "When He comes, He will tell us all things."

²⁶Jesus said to her, "I who speak to you am He."

²⁷And at this point His disciples came, and they marveled that He talked with a woman; yet no one said, "What do You seek?" or, "Why are You talking with her?"

²⁸The woman then left her waterpot, went her way into the city, and said to the men, ²⁹"Come, see a Man who told me all things that I ever did. Could this be the Christ?" ³⁰Then they went out of the city and came to Him.

EXPLORATION

1. What can you conclude about this woman's character?

2. How do you think the woman felt when Jesus talked to her?

3. How did Jesus demonstrate his love for this woman?

4. How did the woman react to her encounter with Jesus?

5. What do the woman's actions reveal about the way Jesus affected her life?

INSPIRATION

Remarkable. Jesus didn't reveal the secret to King Herod. He didn't request an audience of the Sanhedrin and tell them the news. It wasn't within the colonnades of a Roman court that he announced his identity.

No, it was in the shade of a well in a rejected land to an ostracized woman. His eyes must have danced as he whispered the secret.

"I am the Messiah."

The most important phrase in the chapter is one easily overlooked. "Then, leaving her water jar, the woman went back to the town and said to the people, 'Come, see a man who told me everything I ever did. Could this be the Christ?'"

Don't miss the drama of the moment. Look at her eyes, wide with amazement. Listen to her as she struggles for words. "Y-y-y-you a-a-a-are the M-m-m-messiah!" And watch as she scrambles to her feet, takes one last look at this grinning Nazarene, turns and runs right into the burly chest of Peter. She almost falls, regains her balance, and hotfoots it toward her hometown.

Did you notice what she forgot? She forgot her water jar. She left behind the jug that had caused the sag in her shoulders. She left behind the burden she brought.

Suddenly the shame of the tattered romances disappeared. Suddenly the insignificance of her life was swallowed by the significance of the moment. "God is here! God has come! God cares . . . for me!"

That is why she forgot her water jar. That is why she ran to the city. That is why she grabbed the first person she saw and announced her discovery, "I just talked to a man who knows everything I ever did . . . and he loves me anyway!"

The disciples offered Jesus some food. He refused it—he was too excited! He had just done what he does best. He had taken a life that was drifting and given it direction.

He was exuberant!

"Look!" he announced to the disciples, pointing at the woman who was running to the village. "Vast fields of human souls are ripening all around us, and are ready now for the reaping." (From *Six Hours One Friday* by Max Lucado)

REACTION

6. In what ways can you identify with the woman in this story?

7. What does this story reveal about God's attitude toward sinful people?

8. When have you felt God's concern and love for you?

9. What keeps you from showing God's love to others?

10. How does the woman's response to Jesus inspire you?

11. How do Jesus' actions in this story encourage you to treat others?

LIFE LESSONS

When we least expect him in our lives, Jesus shows up. Sometimes when we are actively trying to avoid anything that would remind us that our lives are not as they should be, we find Jesus waiting in the very place we have run to hide. Jesus never forces himself on us, but he does have an uncanny way of interrupting our thoughts and actions with truthful questions and challenging ideas. Think about the times Jesus has showed up in your life, as a way of starting a life-changing episode with you.

DEVOTION

Father, your Word assures us that no one is beyond hope. You accept and love each one of us, in spite of our failures. You offer us salvation. You offer us mercy. You offer us love. Thank you for intervening in our lives and rescuing us from the bondage of sin. We praise you for your mercy, forgiveness, and love.

For more Bible passages on God's mercy and love for sinners, see Exodus 34:6; Deuteronomy 4:31; Luke 1:50; 19:1–10; John 3:16; 8:3–11; Ephesians 2:1–6.

To complete the book of John during this twelve-part study, read John 3:1–4:42.

JOURNALING

How can I reach out to others as Jesus did?

L E S S O N   F O U R

HEALING
THE SICK

MAX
LUCADO

REFLECTION

There are many hurting people in our society. The poor, the sick, the homeless, the incarcerated.. There are people with inner wounds: the grieving, the lonely, the depressed. All too often they are not only forgotten but also invisible. Think about the people in your sphere of influence. How can you take notice? To whom can you be a help and support this week?

SITUATION

Jerusalem drew Jews to gather throughout the year. Most came for three major feasts/holidays. Some came on healing pilgrimages, expecting to find wholeness in the city of David. Miracles were connected with the waters of the pool of Bethesda. But the man in this lesson's passage was unable to get in the waters, even though he had spent years near the pool. Jesus took time out from his Sabbath to speak to this man.

BOOK OF JOHN

OBSERVATION

Read John 5:1–5 from the NCV or the NKJV.

NCV

¹Later Jesus went to Jerusalem for a special Jewish feast. ²In Jerusalem there is a pool with five covered porches, which is called Bethzatha in the Jewish language. This pool is near the Sheep Gate. ³Many sick people were lying on the porches beside the pool. Some were blind, some were crippled, and some were paralyzed. ⁵A man was lying there who had been sick for thirty-eight years. ⁶When Jesus saw the man and knew that he had been sick for such a long time, Jesus asked him, "Do you want to be well?"

⁷The sick man answered, "Sir, there is no one to help me get into the pool when the water starts moving. While I am coming to the water, someone else always gets in before me."

⁸Then Jesus said, "Stand up. Pick up your mat and walk." ⁹And immediately the man was well; he picked up his mat and began to walk.

The day this happened was a Sabbath day. ¹⁰So the Jews said to the man who had been healed, "Today is the Sabbath. It is against our law for you to carry your mat on the Sabbath day."

¹¹But he answered, "The man who made me well told me, 'Pick up your mat and walk.'"

¹²Then they asked him, "Who is the man who told you to pick up your mat and walk?"

¹³But the man who had been healed did not know who it was, because there were many people in that place, and Jesus had left.

¹⁴Later, Jesus found the man at the Temple and said to him, "See, you are well now. Stop sinning so that something worse does not happen to you."

¹⁵Then the man left and told the Jews that Jesus was the one who had made him well.

NKJV

¹After this there was a feast of the Jews, and Jesus went up to Jerusalem. ²Now there is in Jerusalem by the Sheep Gate a pool, which is called in Hebrew, Bethesda, having five porches. ³In these lay a great multitude of sick people, blind, lame, paralyzed, waiting for the moving of the water. ⁴For an angel went down at a certain time into the pool and stirred up the water; then whoever stepped in first, after the stirring of the water, was made well of whatever disease he had. ⁵Now a certain man was there who had an infirmity thirty-eight years. ⁶When Jesus saw him lying there, and knew that he already had been in that condition a long time, He said to him, "Do you want to be made well?"

⁷The sick man answered Him, "Sir, I have no man to put me into the pool when the water is stirred up; but while I am coming, another steps down before me."

⁸*Jesus said to him, "Rise, take up your bed and walk."* ⁹*And immediately the man was made well, took up his bed, and walked.*

And that day was the Sabbath. ¹⁰*The Jews therefore said to him who was cured, "It is the Sabbath; it is not lawful for you to carry your bed."*

¹¹*He answered them, "He who made me well said to me, 'Take up your bed and walk.'"*

¹²*Then they asked him, "Who is the Man who said to you, 'Take up your bed and walk'?"* ¹³*But the one who was healed did not know who it was, for Jesus had withdrawn, a multitude being in that place.* ¹⁴*Afterward Jesus found him in the temple, and said to him, "See, you have been made well. Sin no more, lest a worse thing come upon you."*

¹⁵*The man departed and told the Jews that it was Jesus who had made him well.*

EXPLORATION

1. What do you think motivated Jesus to go to Bethzatha (also called Bethesda) during a time of celebration?

2. This story focuses on one invalid man at Bethzatha. What words would you use to describe this man's life?

3. Why do you think Jesus chose to help this particular man?

4. After healing the man, why was it important to Jesus to find him and speak to him again?

5. What do Jesus' actions in this story teach us about his character?

INSPIRATION

It's called Bethesda. It could be called Central Park, Metropolitan Hospital, or even Joe's Bar and Grill. It could be the homeless huddled beneath a downtown overpass. It could be Calvary Baptist. It could be any collection of hurting people.

An underwater spring caused the pool to bubble occasionally. The people believed the bubbles were caused by the dipping of angels' wings. They also believed that the first person to touch the water after the angel did would be healed. Did healing occur? I don't know. But I do know crowds of invalids came to give it a try.

Picture a battleground strewn with wounded bodies, and you see Bethesda. Imagine a nursing home overcrowded and understaffed, and you see the pool. Call to mind the orphans in Bangladesh or the abandoned in New Delhi, and you will see what people saw when they passed Bethesda. As they passed, what did they hear? An endless wave of groans. What did they witness? A field of faceless need. What did they do? Most walked past, ignoring the people.

But not Jesus. He is in Jerusalem for a feast. . . .

He is alone. He is not there to teach the disciples or to draw a crowd. The people need him—so he's there.

Can you picture it? Jesus walking among the suffering.

What is he thinking? When an infected hand touches his ankle, what does he do? When a blind child stumbles in Jesus' path, does he reach down to catch the child? When a wrinkled hand extends for alms, how does Jesus respond?

Whether the watering hole is Bethesda or Bill's Bar . . . how does God feel when people hurt?

It's worth the telling of the story if all we do is watch him walk. It's worth it just to know he even came. He didn't have to, you know. Surely there are more sanitary crowds in Jerusalem. Surely there are more enjoyable activities. After all, this is the Passover feast. It's an exciting time in the holy city. People have come from miles around to meet God in the temple.

Little do they know that God is with the sick.

Little do they know that God is walking slowly, stepping carefully between the beggars and the blind.

Little do they know that the strong young carpenter who surveys the ragged landscape of pain is God. (From *He Still Moves Stones* by Max Lucado)

REACTION

6. How were others affected who witnessed this healing?

7. What are some of the challenges of ministering to people with a serious illness? What are the rewards?

8. How can we demonstrate God's love to people who are suffering?

9. Why is it important for believers to minister to hurting people?

10. Do you know someone who is hurting? How can you reach out to that person?

11. How can we become more sensitive to the suffering of others?

LIFE LESSONS

Jesus went to places where people were hurting. There was intention in his steps. We can claim there are hurting people all around us, but if we are going to live by Jesus' example, we need to make it part of our lifestyle to visit places where people are obviously hurting: prisons, hospitals, disaster areas, nursing homes— the list is pretty obvious. We may not know how we can help, but we will never find that out or discover how God can use us if we avoid the company of suffering people.

DEVOTION

Forgive us, Father, for ignoring the needs of others. Help us respond to the suffering around us. Fill us with your love. Give us your compassion for the hurting, your love for the despised, your mercy for the afflicted.

For more Bible passages about helping the needy, see Matthew 25:34–46; 1 Thessalonians 5:14; Hebrews 6:10–11.

To complete the book of John during this twelve-part study, read John 4:43–5:47.

JOURNALING

How have I felt God's love for me during painful times?

LESSON FIVE

A HUNGRY CROWD

MAX
LUCADO

REFLECTION

At first glance, the need often looks greater than the resources. Five loaves and two fish may seem like an insignificant resource for a crowd, until we place them in the hands of someone who really knows what to do with them. God often take a little gift and makes something great out of it. Think of a time when God provided for your needs in an unusual or surprising way. How did that experience strengthen your faith?

SITUATION

We live in a world of fast-food restaurants and readily available sources of food. We can hardly imagine a crowd of several thousand, hungry and without relief. They have been receiving "spiritual" food in the form of teaching from Jesus, but their physical needs are beginning to distract them. Jesus takes the opportunity to offer his followers a valuable lesson.

OBSERVATION

Read John 6:1–15 from the NCV or the NKJV.

NCV

¹*After this, Jesus went across Lake Galilee (or, Lake Tiberias).* ²*Many people followed him because they saw the miracles he did to heal the sick.* ³*Jesus went up on a hill and sat down there with his followers.* ⁴*It was almost the time for the Jewish Passover Feast.*

⁵*When Jesus looked up and saw a large crowd coming toward him, he said to Philip, "Where can we buy enough bread for all these people to eat?"* ⁶*(Jesus asked Philip this question to test him, because Jesus already knew what he planned to do.)*

⁷*Philip answered, "We would all have to work a month to buy enough bread for each person to have only a little piece."*

⁸*Another one of his followers, Andrew, Simon Peter's brother, said,* ⁹*"Here is a boy with five loaves of barley bread and two little fish, but that is not enough for so many people."*

¹⁰*Jesus said, "Tell the people to sit down." This was a very grassy place, and about five thousand men sat down there.* ¹¹*Then Jesus took the loaves of bread, thanked God for them, and gave them to the people who were sitting there. He did the same with the fish, giving as much as the people wanted.*

¹²*When they had all had enough to eat, Jesus said to his followers, "Gather the leftover pieces of fish and bread so that nothing is wasted."* ¹³*So they gathered up the pieces and filled twelve baskets with the pieces left from the five barley loaves.*

¹⁴*When the people saw this miracle that Jesus did, they said, "He must truly be the Prophet who is coming into the world."*

¹⁵*Jesus knew that the people planned to come and take him by force and make him their king, so he left and went into the hills alone.*

NKJV

After these things Jesus went over the Sea of Galilee, which is the Sea of Tiberias. ²*Then a great multitude followed Him, because they saw His signs which He performed on those who were diseased. And Jesus went up on the mountain, and there He sat with His disciples.*

⁴*Now the Passover, a feast of the Jews, was near.* ⁵*Then Jesus lifted up His eyes, and seeing a great multitude coming toward Him, He said to Philip, "Where shall we buy bread, that these may eat?"* ⁶*But this He said to test him, for He Himself knew what He would do.*

⁷*Philip answered Him, "Two hundred denarii worth of bread is not sufficient for them, that every one of them may have a little."*

⁸*One of His disciples, Andrew, Simon Peter's brother, said to Him,* ⁹*"There is a lad here who has five barley loaves and two small fish, but what are they among so many?"*

[10]Then Jesus said, "Make the people sit down." Now there was much grass in the place. So the men sat down, in number about five thousand. [11]And Jesus took the loaves, and when He had given thanks He distributed them to the disciples, and the disciples to those sitting down; and likewise of the fish, as much as they wanted. [12]So when they were filled, He said to His disciples, "Gather up the fragments that remain, so that nothing is lost." [13]Therefore they gathered them up, and filled twelve baskets with the fragments of the five barley loaves which were left over by those who had eaten. [14]Then those men, when they had seen the sign that Jesus did, said, "This is truly the Prophet who is to come into the world." [15]Therefore when Jesus perceived that they were about to come and take Him by force to make Him king, He departed again to the mountain by Himself alone.

EXPLORATION

1. Why do you think the people went out to see Jesus without bringing along any food? (This event is also described in Matthew 14:13–21, Mark 6:30–44, and Luke 9:10–17.)

2. Why did Jesus ask Philip how they could feed the crowd?

3. What can we learn from Philip's response? What was the larger obstacle for Philip: the lack of food or the costs involved in feeding such a large crowd?

4. What do you think Jesus wanted his disciples to learn from this event?

5. Who are you most like in this story? Philip? Andrew? The boy? The people? Why?

INSPIRATION

Interestingly, the stress seen that day is not on Jesus' face, but on the faces of the disciples. "Send the crowds away," they demand. Fair request. "After all," they are saying, "You've taught them. You've healed them. You've accommodated them. And now they're getting hungry. If we don't send them away, they'll want you to feed them, too!"

I wish I could have seen the expression on the disciples' faces when they heard the Master's response. . . .

"You give them something to eat." . . .

Rather than look to God, they looked in their wallets. "That would take eight months of a man's wages! Are we to go and spend that much on bread and give it to them to eat?"

"Y-y-y-you've got to be kidding."

"He can't be serious."

"It's one of Jesus' jokes."

"Do you know how many people are out there?"

Eyes watermelon wide. Jaws dangling open. One ear hearing the din of the crowd, the other the command of God.

Don't miss the contrasting views. When Jesus saw the people, he saw an opportunity to love and affirm value. When the disciples saw the people they saw thousands of problems.

Also, don't miss the irony. In the midst of a bakery—in the presence of the Eternal Baker—they tell the "Bread of Life" that there is no bread.

How silly we must appear to God.

Here's where Jesus should have given up. This is the point in the pressure-packed day where Jesus should have exploded. The sorrow, the life threats, the exuberance, the crowds, the interruptions, the demands, and now this. His own disciples can't do what he asks them. In front of five thousand men, they let him down.

"Beam me up, Father," should have been Jesus' next words. But they weren't. Instead he inquires, "How many loaves do you have?"

The disciples bring him a little boy's lunch. A lunch pail becomes a banquet, and all are fed. No word of reprimand is given. No furrowed brow of anger is seen. No "I-told-you-so" speech is delivered. The same compassion Jesus extends to the crowd is extended to his friends. (From *In the Eye of the Storm* by Max Lucado)

REACTION

6. What problems in your life seem to have no solutions?

7. Do you find it difficult to trust God to meet your needs? Why?

8. What does this story teach us about the way God provides for his people?

9. In what ways has God given you wisdom and strength to overcome difficulties in your life?

10. Based on this event, how do you think God wants you to deal with your doubts?

11. How does the faith of other believers inspire us to trust God?

LIFE LESSONS

It's never about how much we have to offer, but rather if we will offer whatever we have. Jesus had the power to create food out of thin air or from the rocks on the hillside. He chose to work with a small gift from a little boy. Sometimes the greatest miracle happens when we let go of some little possession and put it into God's hands. What God does with what we give him becomes secondary to the delight of participating in his work in the world.

DEVOTION

Father, why do we doubt you? Time and time again, you have proved your faithfulness, yet our faith falters. Thank you for continually providing for our needs. Keep us from doubt. Fill us with faith in you. Remind us that you are bigger than all of our problems and needs.

For more Bible passages on God's provision for his people, see Genesis 2:15–16; Exodus 16:1–31; Psalm 20:7; Proverbs 3:5–10; Matthew 6:25–34.

To complete the book of John during this twelve-part study, read John 6:1–71.

JOURNALING

What keeps me from trusting God to meet my needs?

LESSON SIX

A GUILTY
WOMAN

MAX
LUCADO

REFLECTION

The longing for love and acceptance that makes us human can also lead us to make shameful and sad choices. Even more shocking are some of the thoughtless and evil acts people commit toward others they deem less worthy of love. Yet each of us desires those marvelous moments when we feel valued and appreciated by someone else. What are some responses or gestures that make you feel loved and accepted by others?

SITUATION

John includes this brief episode in his Gospel as an illustration of the lengths some people went to, in order to trap and destroy Jesus. Certain leaders had already attempted to undermine his position, and efforts had been made to arrest him. They continued to test his orthodoxy with this crude confrontation in which a woman, clearly guilty of an offense, was brought to Jesus. They had little interest in justice. They asked Jesus, "What do you say?" Neither the opponents nor the woman expected the answer Jesus gave.

OBSERVATION

Read John 8:1–11 from the NCV or the NKJV.

NCV

¹Jesus went to the Mount of Olives. ²But early in the morning he went back to the Temple, and all the people came to him, and he sat and taught them. ³The teachers of the law and the Pharisees brought a woman who had been caught in adultery. They forced her to stand before the people. ⁴They said to Jesus, "Teacher, this woman was caught having sexual relations with a man who is not her husband. ⁵The law of Moses commands that we stone to death every woman who does this. What do you say we should do?" ⁶They were asking this to trick Jesus so that they could have some charge against him.

But Jesus bent over and started writing on the ground with his finger. ⁷When they continued to ask Jesus their question, he raised up and said, "Anyone here who has never sinned can throw the first stone at her." ⁸Then Jesus bent over again and wrote on the ground.

⁹Those who heard Jesus began to leave one by one, first the older men and then the others. Jesus was left there alone with the woman standing before him. ¹⁰Jesus raised up again and asked her, "Woman, where are they? Has no one judged you guilty?"

¹¹She answered, "No one, sir."

Then Jesus said, "I also don't judge you guilty. You may go now, but don't sin anymore."

NKJV

¹But Jesus went to the Mount of Olives. ²Now early in the morning He came again into the temple, and all the people came to Him; and He sat down and taught them. ³Then the scribes and Pharisees brought to Him a woman caught in adultery. And when they had set her in the midst, ⁴they said to Him, "Teacher, this woman was caught in adultery, in the very act. ⁵Now Moses, in the law, commanded us that such should be stoned. But what do You say?" ⁶This they said, testing Him, that they might have something of which to accuse Him. But Jesus stooped down and wrote on the ground with His finger, as though He did not hear.

⁷So when they continued asking Him, He raised Himself up and said to them, "He who is without sin among you, let him throw a stone at her first." ⁸And again He stooped down and wrote on the ground. ⁹Then those who heard it, being convicted by their conscience, went out one by one, beginning with the oldest even to the last. And Jesus was left alone, and the woman standing in the midst. ¹⁰When Jesus had raised Himself up and saw no one but the woman, He said to her, "Woman, where are those accusers of yours? Has no one condemned you?"

¹¹She said, "No one, Lord."

And Jesus said to her, "Neither do I condemn you; go and sin no more."

EXPLORATION

1. Why did the religious leaders bring the adulterous woman to Jesus? (See Leviticus 20:10 and Deuteronomy 22:22 for the Old Testament background of their charges.)

2. How was Jesus' attitude toward the woman different from the crowd's attitude?

3. Why do you think the older men were the first to leave the scene?

4. With which group or person in the story do you identify?

5. What words would you use to describe the way Jesus treated the guilty woman? How did he address her sin?

INSPIRATION

Sightless and heartless redeemers. Redeemers without power. That's not the Redeemer of the New Testament.

Jesus sits surrounded by a horseshoe of listeners. Some nod their heads in agreement and open their hearts in obedience. They have accepted the teacher as their teacher and are learning to accept him as their Lord.

We don't know his topic that morning. Prayer, perhaps. Or maybe kindness or anxiety. But whatever it was, it was soon interrupted when people burst into the courtyard.

Determined, they erupt out of a narrow street and stomp toward Jesus. The listeners scramble to get out of the way. The mob is made up of religious leaders, the elders and deacons of their day. Respected and important men. And struggling to keep her balance on the crest of this angry wave is a scantily-clad woman.

Only moments before she had been in bed with a man who was not her husband. Was this how she made her living? Maybe. Maybe not. We don't know.

But we do know that a door was jerked open and she was yanked from a bed. She barely had time to cover her body before she was dragged into the street by two men the age of her father.

And now, with holy strides, the mob storms toward the teacher. They throw the woman in his direction. She nearly falls.

"We found this woman in bed with a man!" cries the leader. "The law says to stone her. What do you say?"

In her despair she looks at the Teacher. His eyes don't glare. "Don't worry," they whisper, "it's okay." And for the first time that morning she sees kindness.

As Jesus looked at this daughter, did his mind race back? Did he relive the act of forming this child in heaven? Did he see her as he had originally made her?

So, with the tenderness only a father can have, he set out to untie the knots and repair the holes.

He begins by diverting the crowd's attention. He draws on the ground. Everybody looks down. The woman feels relief as the eyes of the men look away from her.

The accusers are persistent. "Tell us, teacher! What do you want us to do with her?"

He just raised his head and offered an invitation, "I guess if you've never made a mistake, then you have a right to stone this woman." He looked back down and began to draw on the earth again.

Someone cleared his throat as if to speak, but no one spoke. Feet shuffled. Eyes dropped. Then thud . . . thud . . . thud . . . rocks fell to the ground.

And they walked away. They came as one, but they left one by one.

Jesus told the woman to look up. "Is there no one to condemn you?"

Maybe she expected him to scold her. Perhaps she expected him to walk away from her. I'm not sure, but I do know this: What she got, she never expected. She got a promise and a commission.

The promise: "Then neither do I condemn you."

The commission: "Go and sin no more."

The woman turns and walks into anonymity. She's never seen or heard from again. But we can be confident of one thing: On that morning in Jerusalem, she saw Jesus and Jesus saw her. And could we somehow transport her to Rio de Janeiro and let her stand at the base of the *Cristo redentor*, I know what her response would be.

"That's not the Jesus I saw," she would say. For the Jesus she saw didn't have a hard heart. And the Jesus that saw her didn't have blind eyes.

However, if we could somehow transport her to Calvary and let her stand at the base of the cross . . . you know what she would say. "That's him."

She would recognize his voice. It's raspier and weaker, but the words are the same, "Father, forgive them . . ." And she would recognize his eyes. How could she ever forget those eyes? Clear and tear-filled. Eyes that saw her not as she was, but as she was intended to be. (From *Six Hours One Friday* by Max Lucado)

REACTION

6. How does Jesus' interaction with this sinful woman encourage you?

7. What was the attitude of the religious leaders toward the woman? Toward Jesus?

8. How can we avoid these same attitudes?

9. What does this passage reveal about God's view of sin?

10. Why do you think we rank some sins as being far worse than others?

11. How does this passage challenge your attitude about people caught in certain sins?

LIFE LESSONS

God loves with an informed passion. Jesus didn't look at that woman as a stranger for whom he could practice mercy. In his look she met someone who knew exactly who she was and what she had done. And yet, despite his awareness, Jesus did not treat her as an object to make a point or a pawn to manipulate. He spoke the truth. And he set her free to go and sin no more. No matter how often we come to Christ, burdened and fallen again, he is willing to say to us, "Go, and sin no more."

DEVOTION

Father, you are compassionate and forgiving. Like the woman in this story, we stand amazed that you would have such mercy on us. We thank you for your unconditional love. We are not what we should be, but we accept your forgiveness and claim your salvation.

For more Bible passages on God's forgiveness, see Exodus 34:6–7; Deuteronomy 4:31; Luke 1:50; Acts 10:43; Ephesians 1:7; 2:4–5; 1 John 1:8–9.

To complete the book of John during this twelve-part study, read John 7:1–8:59.

JOURNALING

For what sinful attitudes or actions do I need to ask God's forgiveness?

LESSON SEVEN

A MAN
BORN BLIND

MAX
LUCADO

REFLECTION

We all are born with disabilities, whether they be physical or emotional or spiritual ones. The hard part is admitting it and letting God use them. Think about your personal strengths and weaknesses. How has God worked through your weaknesses for his glory?

SITUATION

If you have additional time, consider reading the entire chapter of John 9. The incident begins with a theological question from the disciples, but it quickly escalates into a major confrontation over the rules of the Sabbath. Notice the way human beings develop a distorted view of God when they limit his actions or inflate his commandments.

OBSERVATION

Read John 9:1–12 from the NCV or the NKJV.

NCV

¹*As Jesus was walking along, he saw a man who had been born blind. ²His followers asked him, "Teacher, whose sin caused this man to be born blind—his own sin or his parents' sin?"*

³*Jesus answered, "It is not this man's sin or his parents' sin that made him be blind. This man was born blind so that God's power could be shown in him. ⁴While it is daytime, we must continue doing the work of the One who sent me. Night is coming, when no one can work. ⁵While I am in the world, I am the light of the world."*

[6]*After Jesus said this, he spit on the ground and made some mud with it and put the mud on the man's eyes. [7]Then he told the man, "Go and wash in the Pool of Siloam." (Siloam means Sent.) So the man went, washed, and came back seeing.*

[8]*The neighbors and some people who had earlier seen this man begging said, "Isn't this the same man who used to sit and beg?"*

[9]*Some said, "He is the one," but others said, "No, he only looks like him." The man himself said, "I am the man."*

[10]*They asked, "How did you get your sight?"*

[11]*He answered, "The man named Jesus made some mud and put it on my eyes. Then he told me to go to Siloam and wash. So I went and washed, and then I could see."*

[12]*They asked him, "Where is this man?" "I don't know," he answered.*

NKJV

[1]*Now as Jesus passed by, He saw a man who was blind from birth. [2]And His disciples asked Him, saying, "Rabbi, who sinned, this man or his parents, that he was born blind?"*

[3]*Jesus answered, "Neither this man nor his parents sinned, but that the works of God should be revealed in him. [4]I must work the works of Him who sent Me while it is day; the night is coming when no one can work. [5]As long as I am in the world, I am the light of the world."*

[6]*When He had said these things, He spat on the ground and made clay with the saliva; and He anointed the eyes of the blind man with the clay. [7]And He said to him, "Go, wash in the pool of Siloam" (which is translated, Sent). So he went and washed, and came back seeing.*

[8]*Therefore the neighbors and those who previously had seen that he was blind said, "Is not this he who sat and begged?"*

[9]*Some said, "This is he." Others said, "He is like him." He said, "I am he."*

[10]*Therefore they said to him, "How were your eyes opened?"*

[11]*He answered and said, "A Man called Jesus made clay and anointed my eyes and said to me, 'Go to the pool of Siloam and wash.' So I went and washed, and I received sight."*

[12]*Then they said to him, "Where is He?"*

He said, "I do not know."

EXPLORATION

1. What assumptions did Jesus' followers make about this man's blindness?

2. What misconception did Jesus correct?

3. How did Jesus involve the blind man in the healing process?

4. Why do you think Jesus sent the man to wash in a pool before he healed him?

5. How did the people of the town respond to the miracle?

INSPIRATION

What about the blind man Jesus and the disciples discovered? The followers thought he was a great theological case study.

"Why do you think he's blind?" one asked.

"He must have sinned."

"No, it's his folks' fault."

"Jesus, what do you think? Why is he blind?"

"He's blind to show what God can do."

The apostles knew what was coming; they had seen this look in Jesus' eyes before. They knew what he was going to do, but they didn't know how he was going to do it. "Lightning? Thunder? A shout? A clap of the hands?" They all watched.

Jesus began to work his mouth a little. The onlookers stared. "What is he doing?" He moved his jaw as if he were chewing on something.

Some of the people began to get restless. Jesus just chewed. His jaw rotated around until he had what he wanted. Spit. Ordinary saliva.

If no one said it, somebody had to be thinking it: "Yuk!"

Jesus spat on the ground, stuck his finger into the puddle, and stirred. Soon it was a mud pie, and he smeared some of the mud across the blind man's eyes.

The same One who'd turned a stick into a scepter and a pebble into a missile now turned saliva and mud into a balm for the blind.

Once again, the mundane became majestic. Once again the dull became divine, the humdrum holy. Once again God's power was seen, not through the ability of the instrument, but through its availability.

"Blessed are the meek," Jesus explained. Blessed are the available. Blessed are the conduits, the tunnels, the tools. Deliriously joyful are the ones who believe that if God has used sticks, rocks, and spit to do his will, then he can use us. (From *The Applause of Heaven* by Max Lucado)

REACTION

6. What can we learn from responses of the blind man and the townspeople to Jesus?

7. If you had been one of the townspeople, how do you think you would have responded?

8. When have you seen a person's weakness or disability used for God's glory?

9. What fresh insight have you gained from this passage about the struggles of life?

10. How do you need to change your attitude toward your personal weaknesses and strengths?

11. Why does God choose to use our weaknesses and problems to bring glory to himself?

LIFE LESSONS

We find it difficult to trust God when we can't figure out why he would allow certain uncomfortable things to happen to us. Interestingly, we don't seem to wonder about God when he allows good things into our lives. One of the life lessons in this man's experience is the reminder that no matter how long we've known Christ, we will never get over the fact that he knew us long before we knew him, and that we will never reach the end of discovering more about him.

DEVOTION

We pray, O Father, that you would increase our faith. Forgive us for doubting your ability to use us for your glory. Forgive us for demanding proof instead of simply believing in you. Use all that we have to accomplish your purposes.

For more Bible passages on being used by God, see Exodus 3:7–4:12; Joshua 1:1–9; Romans 8:26; 1 Corinthians 1:26–28; 2 Corinthians 12:7–10; 2 Timothy 2:21.

To complete the book of John during this twelve-part study, read John 9:1–10:42.

JOURNALING

How can God use my weaknesses or problems for his glory?

THE LOSS OF
A FRIEND

MAX
LUCADO

REFLECTION

For the most part, losses are not an enjoyable part of life. And losing friends is particularly sad. God's presence in our lives ought to cast a slightly different light on losses—especially those that are caused by death. Why? Because death does not limit God's power. If we can trust him to bring good out of even matters of life and death, can we not learn to trust him with smaller losses? Think of a time in your life when a bad experience turned out for good. How did that affect you?

SITUATION

Lazarus's sisters sent word to Jesus that their brother was sick. This was a family that was very close to Jesus and in whose home he had stayed many times. Yet Jesus deliberately delayed. It had taken time to track down Jesus with the news. Then he waited an extra two days. The travel from Perea to Bethany also took time. By the time Jesus arrived, Lazarus was dead and buried.

OBSERVATION

Read John 11:17–44 from the NCV or the NKJV.

NCV

¹⁷When Jesus arrived, he learned that Lazarus had already been dead and in the tomb for four days. ¹⁸Bethany was about two miles from Jerusalem. ¹⁹Many of the Jews had come there to comfort Martha and Mary about their brother.

²⁰When Martha heard that Jesus was coming, she went out to meet him, but Mary stayed home. ²¹Martha said to Jesus, "Lord, if you had been here, my brother would not have died. ²²But I know that even now God will give you anything you ask."

²³Jesus said, "Your brother will rise and live again."

²⁴Martha answered, "I know that he will rise and live again in the resurrection on the last day."

²⁵Jesus said to her, "I am the resurrection and the life. Those who believe in me will have life even if they die. ²⁶And everyone who lives and believes in me will never die. Martha, do you believe this?"

²⁷Martha answered, "Yes, Lord. I believe that you are the Christ, the Son of God, the One coming to the world."

²⁸After Martha said this, she went back and talked to her sister Mary alone. Martha said, "The Teacher is here and he is asking for you." ²⁹When Mary heard this, she got up quickly and went to Jesus. ³⁰Jesus had not yet come into the town but was still at the place where Martha had met him. ³¹The Jews were with Mary in the house, comforting her. When they saw her stand and leave quickly, they followed her, thinking she was going to the tomb to cry there. ³²But Mary went to the place where Jesus was. When she saw him, she fell at his feet and said, "Lord, if you had been here, my brother would not have died."

³³When Jesus saw Mary crying and the Jews who came with her also crying, he was upset and was deeply troubled. ³⁴He asked, "Where did you bury him?" "Come and see, Lord," they said. ³⁵Jesus cried. ³⁶So the Jews said, "See how much he loved him."

³⁷But some of them said, "If Jesus opened the eyes of the blind man, why couldn't he keep Lazarus from dying? " ³⁸Again feeling very upset, Jesus came to the tomb. It was a cave with a large stone covering the entrance. ³⁹Jesus said, "Move the stone away." Martha, the sister of the dead man, said, "But, Lord, it has been four days since he died. There will be a bad smell." ⁴⁰Then Jesus said to her, "Didn't I tell you that if you believed you would see the glory of God?"

⁴¹So they moved the stone away from the entrance. Then Jesus looked up and said, "Father, I thank you that you heard me. ⁴²I know that you always hear me, but I said these things because of the people here around me. I want them to believe that you sent me." ⁴³After Jesus said this, he cried out in a loud voice, "Lazarus, come out!" ⁴⁴The dead man came out, his hands and feet wrapped with pieces of cloth, and a cloth

around his face. Jesus said to them, "Take the cloth off of him and let him go."

NKJV

[17]So when Jesus came, He found that he had already been in the tomb four days. [18]Now Bethany was near Jerusalem, about two miles away. [19]And many of the Jews had joined the women around Martha and Mary, to comfort them concerning their brother.

[20]Now Martha, as soon as she heard that Jesus was coming, went and met Him, but Mary was sitting in the house. [21]Then Martha said to Jesus, "Lord, if You had been here, my brother would not have died. [22]But even now I know that whatever You ask of God, God will give You."

[23]Jesus said to her, "Your brother will rise again."

[24]Martha said to Him, "I know that he will rise again in the resurrection at the last day." [25]Jesus said to her, "I am the resurrection and the life. He who believes in Me, though he may die, he shall live. [26]And whoever lives and believes in Me shall never die. Do you believe this?" [27]She said to Him, "Yes, Lord, I believe that You are the Christ, the Son of God, who is to come into the world."

[28]And when she had said these things, she went her way and secretly called Mary her sister, saying, "The Teacher has come and is calling for you." [29]As soon as she heard that, she arose quickly and came to Him. [30]Now Jesus had not yet come into the town, but was in the place where Martha met Him. [31]Then the Jews who were with her in the house, and comforting her, when they saw that Mary rose up quickly and went out, followed her, saying, "She is going to the tomb to weep there."

[32]Then, when Mary came where Jesus was, and saw Him, she fell down at His feet, saying to Him, "Lord, if You had been here, my brother would not have died." [33]Therefore, when Jesus saw her weeping, and the Jews who came with her weeping, He groaned in the spirit and was troubled. [34]And He said, "Where have you laid him?" They said to Him, "Lord, come and see."

[35]Jesus wept. [36]Then the Jews said, "See how He loved him!" [37]And some of them said, "Could not this Man, who opened the eyes of the blind, also have kept this man from dying?"

[38]Then Jesus, again groaning in Himself, came to the tomb. It was a cave, and a stone lay against it. [39]Jesus said, "Take away the stone." Martha, the sister of him who was dead, said to Him, "Lord, by this time there is a stench, for he has been dead four days."

[40]Jesus said to her, "Did I not say to you that if you would believe you would see the glory of God?" [41]Then they took away the stone from the place where the dead man was lying. And Jesus lifted up His eyes and said, "Father, I thank You that You have heard Me. [42]And I know that You always hear Me, but because of the people who are standing by I said this, that they may believe that You sent Me." [43]Now when He had said these things, He cried with a loud voice, "Lazarus, come forth!" [44]And he who had died came

out bound hand and foot with graveclothes, and his face was wrapped with a cloth. Jesus said to them, "Loose him, and let him go."

EXPLORATION

1. How did Mary and Martha feel about Jesus' late arrival?

2. How did Mary and Martha differ in the way they expressed their feelings?

3. Do you think Jesus' words to Martha were reassuring to her? Why or why not?

4. How did Martha communicate her belief in Jesus?

5. How did Jesus respond to Mary, Martha, and the others' mourning?

INSPIRATION

Have you been there? Have you been called to stand at the thin line that separates the living from the dead? Have you lain awake at night listening to machines pumping air in and out of your lungs? Have you watched sickness corrode and atrophy the body of a friend? Have you lingered behind at the cemetery long after the others have left, gazing in disbelief at the metal casket that contains the body that contained the soul of the one you can't believe is gone? If so, then this canyon is not unfamiliar to you . . .

In this scene there are two people: Martha and Jesus. And for all practical purposes they are the only two people in the universe. Her words were full of despair. "If you had been here . . ." She stares into the Master's face with confused eyes. She'd been strong long enough; now it hurt too badly. Lazarus was dead. Her brother was gone. And the one man who could have made a difference didn't. He hadn't even made it for the burial. Something about death makes us accuse God of betrayal. "If God were here there would be no death!" we claim . . .

Jesus wasn't angry at Martha. Perhaps it was his patience that caused her to change her tone from frustration to earnestness. "Even now God will give you whatever you ask."

Jesus then made one of those claims that place him either on the throne or in the asylum: "Your brother will rise again."

Martha misunderstood. (Who wouldn't have?) "I know he will rise again in the resurrection at the last day."

That wasn't what Jesus meant. Don't miss the context of the next words. Imagine the setting: Jesus has intruded on the enemy's turf; he's standing in Satan's territory, Death Canyon. His stomach turns as he smells the sulfuric stench of the ex-angel, and he winces as he hears the oppressed wails of those trapped in the prison. Satan has been here. He has violated one of God's creations.

With his foot planted on the serpent's head, Jesus speaks loudly enough that his words echo off the canyon walls.

"I am the resurrection and the life. He who believes in me will live, even though he dies; and whoever lives and believes in me will never die" (John 11:25).

It is the hinge point in history. A chink has been found in death's armor. The keys to the halls of hell have been claimed . . . With eyes locked on hers he asks the greatest question found in Scripture, a question meant as much for you and me as for Martha.

"Do you believe this?"

Wham! There it is. The bottom line. The dimension that separates Jesus from a thousand gurus and prophets who have come down the pike. The question that drives any responsible listener to absolute obedience or to total rejection of the Christian faith.

"Do you believe this?"

Let the question sink into your heart for a minute. Do you believe that a young, penniless itinerant is larger than your death? Do you truly believe that death is nothing more than an entrance ramp to a new highway? . . .

This is a canyon question. A question which makes sense only during an all-night vigil or in the stillness of smoke-filled waiting rooms. A question that makes sense when all of our props, crutches, and costumes are taken away. For then we must face ourselves as we really are: rudderless humans tailspinning toward disaster. And we are forced to see him for what he claims to be: our only hope. (From God Came Near by Max Lucado)

REACTION

6. How did Martha's response demonstrate both faith and a lack of faith?

7. How do Jesus' words and actions in this passage comfort you?

8. How has God helped you during a sad or disappointing time?

9. How can you share the pain of others who suffer?

LIFE LESSONS

Grief often spawns blame. Tiny fingerlings of fault suggest themselves to us. Someone we love dies. Perhaps it was our fault. Maybe it was someone else's fault. It *has* to be someone's fault. And if no appropriate guilty party accepts the blame, then there's always God. We are sometimes so busy assigning blame that we miss the point of death's inevitability and the genuine hope of resurrection. Jesus used the death of one friend and the sorrow of two others to demonstrate for all time that real life is more than this plane of existence, as sweet and wonderful as this one can be. It was not meant to be the whole meal, but a foretaste of things eternal.

DEVOTION

Father, thank you for caring about our pain and disappointments. Calm the whirling winds of fear and hurt that threaten our faith. Keep us from trying to cope with our struggles by our own strength and willpower. Help us to release our emotions to you and trust you to sustain us. Thank you for your comforting words of wisdom. Let us receive the healing of the Holy Spirit.

For more Bible passages dealing with hurts, see Matthew 9:36; 11:28–30; Romans 12:15; 2 Corinthians 1:3–7.

To complete the book of John during this twelve-part study, read John 11:1–12:50.

JOURNALING

How can I surrender past hurts and disappointments to God?

LESSON NINE

THE MASTER
SERVANT

MAX
LUCADO

REFLECTION

Someone has wisely observed that being a servant is fine until someone starts treating you like one. We don't naturally gravitate toward servanthood. Helping others has a certain charm as long as it doesn't inconvenience or cost too much. But genuine servanthood is about being put upon. Authentic service is sparked by the immediate need, not the convenience of energy, schedule, or especially social norms and expectations. Think of a special time when you enjoyed fellowship with other believers. What aspects of service can you identify in that setting? How did the presence of service cause you to enjoy that fellowship so much?

SITUATION

On the night he was betrayed, Jesus said and did many things. He stayed on message and on task. He was about to show his disciples how much he loved them by dying for them. But before that, he would demonstrate how much he loved them in a simple, practical, profound way.

OBSERVATION

Read John 13:1–20 from the NCV or the NKJV.

NCV

¹It was almost time for the Jewish Passover Feast. Jesus knew that it was time for him to leave this world and go back to the Father. He had always loved those who were his own in the world, and he loved them all the way to the end.

²Jesus and his followers were at the evening meal. The devil had already persuaded Judas Iscariot, the son of Simon, to turn against Jesus. ³Jesus knew that the Father had given him power over everything and that he had come from God and was going back to God.

⁴So during the meal Jesus stood up and took off his outer clothing. Taking a towel, he wrapped it around his waist. ⁵Then he poured water into a bowl and began to wash the followers' feet, drying them with the towel that was wrapped around him.

⁶Jesus came to Simon Peter, who said to him, "Lord, are you going to wash my feet?"

⁷Jesus answered, "You don't understand now what I am doing, but you will understand later." ⁸Peter said, "No, you will never wash my feet."

Jesus answered, "If I don't wash your feet, you are not one of my people."

⁹Simon Peter answered, "Lord, then wash not only my feet, but wash my hands and my head, too!"

¹⁰Jesus said, "After a person has had a bath, his whole body is clean. He needs only to wash his feet. And you men are clean, but not all of you." ¹¹Jesus knew who would turn against him, and that is why he said, "Not all of you are clean."

¹²When he had finished washing their feet, he put on his clothes and sat down again. He asked, "Do you understand what I have just done for you? ¹³You call me 'Teacher' and 'Lord,' and you are right, because that is what I am. ¹⁴If I, your Lord and Teacher, have washed your feet, you also should wash each other's feet. ¹⁵I did this as an example so that you should do as I have done for you. ¹⁶I tell you the truth, a servant is not greater than his master. A messenger is not greater than the one who sent him. ¹⁷If you know these things, you will be happy if you do them.

[18] "I am not talking about all of you. I know those I have chosen. But this is to bring about what the Scripture said: 'The man who ate at my table has turned against me.' [19]I am telling you this now before it happens so that when it happens, you will believe that I am he. [20]I tell you the truth, whoever accepts anyone I send also accepts me. And whoever accepts me also accepts the One who sent me."

NKJV

[1]Now before the Feast of the Passover, when Jesus knew that His hour had come that He should depart from this world to the Father, having loved His own who were in the world, He loved them to the end.

[2]And supper being ended, the devil having already put it into the heart of Judas Iscariot, Simon's son, to betray Him, [3]Jesus, knowing that the Father had given all things into His hands, and that He had come from God and was going to God, [4]rose from supper and laid aside His garments, took a towel and girded Himself. [5]After that, He poured water into a basin and began to wash the disciples' feet, and to wipe them with the towel with which He was girded. [6]Then He came to Simon Peter. And Peter said to Him, "Lord, are You washing my feet?"

[7]Jesus answered and said to him, "What I am doing you do not understand now, but you will know after this."

[8]Peter said to Him, "You shall never wash my feet!"

Jesus answered him, "If I do not wash you, you have no part with Me."

[9]Simon Peter said to Him, "Lord, not my feet only, but also my hands and my head!"

[10]Jesus said to him, "He who is bathed needs only to wash his feet, but is completely clean; and you are clean, but not all of you." [11]For He knew who would betray Him; therefore He said, "You are not all clean."

[12]So when He had washed their feet, taken His garments, and sat down again, He said to them, "Do you know what I have done to you? [13]You call Me Teacher and Lord, and you say well, for so I am. [14]If I then, your Lord and Teacher, have washed your feet, you also ought to wash one another's feet. [15]For I have given you an example, that you should do as I have done to you. [16]Most assuredly, I say to you, a servant is not greater than his master; nor is he who is sent greater than he who sent him. [17]If you know these things, blessed are you if you do them.

[18] "I do not speak concerning all of you. I know whom I have chosen; but that the Scripture may be fulfilled, 'He who eats bread with Me has lifted up his heel against Me.' [19]Now I tell you before it comes, that when it does come to pass, you may believe that I am He. [20]Most assuredly, I say to you, he who receives whomever I send receives Me; and he who receives Me receives Him who sent Me."

EXPLORATION

1. What do you suppose the atmosphere was like at this meal?

2. What range of feelings did Jesus have for his disciples?

3. How did Jesus show his love for his friends?

4. What was Simon Peter's immediate reaction to being served by Jesus?

5. Why was it difficult for Simon Peter to accept Jesus' service?

INSPIRATION

It has been a long day. Jerusalem is packed with Passover guests, most of whom clamor for a glimpse of the Teacher. The spring sun is warm. The streets are dry. And the disciples are a long way from home. A splash of cool water would be refreshing.

The disciples enter, one by one, and take their places around the table. On the wall hangs a towel, and on the floor sits a pitcher and a basin. Any one of the disciples could volunteer for the job, but not one does.

After a few moments, Jesus stands and removes his outer garment. He wraps a servant's girdle around his waist, takes up the basin, and kneels before one of the disciples. He unlaces a sandal and gently lifts the foot and places it in the basin, covers it with water, and begins to bathe it. One by one; one grimy foot after another, Jesus works his way down the row.

In Jesus' day the washing of feet was a task reserved not just for servants but for the lowest of servants. Every circle has its pecking order, and the circle of household workers was no exception. The servant at the bottom of the totem pole was expected to be the one on his knees with the towel and basin.

In this case the one with the towel and basin is the King of the universe. Hands that shaped the stars now wash away filth. Fingers that formed mountains now massage toes. And the one before whom all nations will one day kneel now kneels before his disciples. Hours before his own death, Jesus' concern is singular. He wants his disciples to know how much he loves them. More than removing dirt, Jesus is removing doubt. (From *Just Like Jesus* by Max Lucado)

REACTION

6. What long-term impact do you think Jesus' actions had on the disciples?

7. When has the humble service of a fellow believer inspired you?

8. What are some of the rewards of serving others?

9. Why is it important for believers to have fellowship with each other?

10. How does it affect you to see people serving with humility in the church?

11. When have you found it difficult to accept help from a fellow believer? Why?

LIFE LESSONS

What if we serve and no one notices? What if we help and no one seems to care? What if we offer to serve and are rejected? Welcome to a servant's world. Jesus never predicted how the serv*ees* would respond; he simply placed his actions before us as an example. We pray for alertness to opportunities and the wisdom to respond as Jesus would respond. Meanwhile, we learn to express gratitude to Jesus for his immeasurable act of service in going to the cross for us.

DEVOTION

Father, in Jesus we see the perfect model of humble service. Help us to be like him. Open our eyes to the needs of others. Help us to follow your Word. Help us to follow in Christ's footsteps.

For more Bible passages on serving, see Matthew 20:25–28; Ephesians 6:7; Galatians 5:13; Philippians 2:7.

To complete the book of John during this twelve-part study, read John 13:1–14:14.

JOURNALING

What practical things can I do to serve others?

LESSON TEN

JESUS'
PRAYER

MAX
LUCADO

REFLECTION

Hearing someone pray for you by name can have a deep and lasting effect. It's humbling and wonderful to know that someone is actually thinking about you and that your name has been mentioned in God's presence. You can return the favor. Whether or not they hear you, make it a habit to include thoughtful prayer for others when you bow before God. Think for a moment about how you pray for others. What, if anything, needs to change?

SITUATION

The events of John 13 through 17 happened during the Last Supper, on the final evening of Jesus' ministry on earth. In light of his approaching betrayal and death, Jesus prayed for his followers. Although there are many references to Jesus praying throughout the Gospels, this is the longest example of the way Jesus talked with his Father.

OBSERVATION

Read John 17:1–26 from the NCV or the NKJV.

NCV

¹After Jesus said these things, he looked toward heaven and prayed, "Father, the time has come. Give glory to your Son so that the Son can give glory to you. ²You gave the Son power over all people so that the Son could give eternal life to all those you gave him. ³And this is eternal life: that people know you, the only true God, and that they know Jesus Christ, the One you sent. ⁴Having finished the work you gave me to do, I brought you glory on earth. ⁵And now, Father, give me glory with you; give me the glory I had with you before the world was made.

⁶"I showed what you are like to those you gave me from the world. They belonged to you, and you gave them to me, and they have obeyed your teaching. ⁷Now they know that everything you gave me comes from you. ⁸I gave them the teachings you gave me, and they accepted them. They knew that I truly came from you, and they believed that you sent me. ⁹I am praying for them. I am not praying for people in the world but for those you gave me, because they are yours. ¹⁰All I have is yours, and all you have is mine. And my glory is shown through them. ¹¹I am coming to you; I will not stay in the world any longer. But they are still in the world. Holy Father, keep them safe by the power of your name, the name you gave me, so that they will be one, just as you and I are one. ¹²While I was with them, I kept them safe by the power of your name, the name you gave me. I protected them, and only one of them, the one worthy of destruction, was lost so that the Scripture would come true.

¹³"I am coming to you now. But I pray these things while I am still in the world so that these followers can have all of my joy in them. ¹⁴I have given them your teaching. And the world has hated them, because they don't belong to the world, just as I don't belong to the world. ¹⁵I am not asking you to take them out of the world but to keep them safe from the Evil One. ¹⁶They don't belong to the world, just as I don't belong to the world. ¹⁷Make them ready for your service through your truth; your teaching is truth. ¹⁸I have sent them into the world, just as you sent me into the world. ¹⁹For their sake, I am making myself ready to serve so that they can be ready for their service of the truth.

²⁰"I pray for these followers, but I am also praying for all those who will believe in me because of their teaching. ²¹Father, I pray that they can be one. As you are in me and I am in you, I pray that they can also be one in us. Then the world will believe that you sent me. ²²I have given these people the glory that you gave me so that they can be one, just as you and I are one. ²³I will be in them and you will be in me so that they will be completely one. Then the world will know that you sent me and that you loved them just as much as you loved me.

²⁴"Father, I want these people that you gave me to be with me where I am. I want them to see my glory, which you gave me because you loved me before the world was made. ²⁵Father, you are the One who is good. The world does not know you, but I know you, and these people know you sent me. ²⁶I showed them what you are like, and I will show them again. Then they will have the same love that you have for me, and I will live in them."

NKJV

¹Jesus spoke these words, lifted up His eyes to heaven, and said: "Father, the hour has come. Glorify Your Son, that Your Son also may glorify You, ²as You have given Him authority over all flesh, that He should give eternal life to as many as You have given Him. ³And this is eternal life, that they may know You, the only true God, and Jesus Christ whom You have sent. ⁴I have glorified You on the earth. I have finished the work which You have given Me to do. ⁵And now, O Father, glorify Me together with Yourself, with the glory which I had with You before the world was.

6 "I have manifested Your name to the men whom You have given Me out of the world. They were Yours, You gave them to Me, and they have kept Your word. 7Now they have known that all things which You have given Me are from You. 8For I have given to them the words which You have given Me; and they have received them, and have known surely that I came forth from You; and they have believed that You sent Me.

9 "I pray for them. I do not pray for the world but for those whom You have given Me, for they are Yours. 10And all Mine are Yours, and Yours are Mine, and I am glorified in them. 11Now I am no longer in the world, but these are in the world, and I come to You. Holy Father, keep through Your name those whom You have given Me, that they may be one as We are. 12While I was with them in the world, I kept them in Your name. Those whom You gave Me I have kept; and none of them is lost except the son of perdition, that the Scripture might be fulfilled. 13But now I come to You, and these things I speak in the world, that they may have My joy fulfilled in themselves. 14I have given them Your word; and the world has hated them because they are not of the world, just as I am not of the world. 15I do not pray that You should take them out of the world, but that You should keep them from the evil one. 16They are not of the world, just as I am not of the world. 17Sanctify them by Your truth. Your word is truth. 18As You sent Me into the world, I also have sent them into the world. 19And for their sakes I sanctify Myself, that they also may be sanctified by the truth.

20 "I do not pray for these alone, but also for those who will believe in Me through their word; 21that they all may be one, as You, Father, are in Me, and I in You; that they also may be one in Us, that the world may believe that You sent Me. 22And the glory which You gave Me I have given them, that they may be one just as We are one: 23I in them, and You in Me; that they may be made perfect in one, and that the world may know that You have sent Me, and have loved them as You have loved Me.

24 "Father, I desire that they also whom You gave Me may be with Me where I am, that they may behold My glory which You have given Me; for You loved Me before the foundation of the world. 25O righteous Father! The world has not known You, but I have known You; and these have known that You sent Me. 26And I have declared to them Your name, and will declare it, that the love with which You loved Me may be in them, and I in them."

EXPLORATION

1. For whom did Jesus pray?

2. How does this prayer depict Jesus' relationship with God the Father?

3. What does Jesus desire for his followers?

4. What spiritual battle is described in Jesus' prayer?

5. How are believers equipped for this battle?

INSPIRATION

Why do Jesus and his angels rejoice over one repenting sinner? Can they see something we can't? Do they know something we don't? Absolutely. They know what heaven holds. They've seen the table, and they've heard the music, and they can't wait to see your face when you arrive. Better still, they can't wait to see you.

When you arrive and enter the party, something wonderful will happen. A final transformation will occur. You will be just like Jesus. Drink deeply from 1 John 3:2 (NCV): "We have not yet been shown what we will be in the future. But we know that when Christ comes again, *we* will be like him" (emphasis mine).

Of all the blessings of heaven, one of the greatest will be you! You will be God's magnum opus, his work of art. The angels will gasp. God's work will be completed. At last, you will have a heart like his.

You will love with a perfect love.

You will worship with a radiant face.

You'll hear each word God speaks.

Your heart will be pure, your words will be like jewels, your thoughts will be like treasures.

You will be just like Jesus. You will, at long last, have a heart like his. Envision the heart of Jesus and you'll be envisioning your own. Guiltless. Fearless. Thrilled and joyous. Tirelessly worshipping. Flawlessly discerning. As the mountain stream is pristine and endless, so will be your heart. *You will be like him.*

And if that were not enough, everyone else will be like him as well . . .

Heaven is populated by those who let God change them. Arguments will cease, for jealousy won't exist. Suspicions won't surface, for there will be no secrets. Every sin is gone. Every insecurity is forgotten. Every fear is past. Pure wheat. No weeds. Pure gold. No alloy. Pure love. No lust. Pure hope. No fear. No wonder the angels rejoice when one sinner repents; they know another work of art will soon grace the gallery of God. They know what heaven holds. (From *Just Like Jesus* by Max Lucado)

REACTION

6. List some of the daily pressures you face. Rank them from 1 to 10 (1 being lightest; 10 being heaviest).

7. How does Jesus' prayer encourage you to face those pressures?

8. What can you learn from this passage about the purpose and practice of prayer?

9. What interferes with your prayer life?

10. How can we overcome feelings of discouragement when our prayers seem to go unanswered?

11. How can prayer affect our lives and the lives of others around us?

LIFE LESSONS

If you are a follower of Jesus Christ, you are an answer to his long-ago prayer. You are one of those who have believed because of the faithfulness of others. There is an unbroken chain of witnesses from that upper room to your heart and mind, just as he expected in prayer. The faith is in your hands, in your life. Ironically, you keep it by giving it away. If you hold it privately and secretly, you haven't kept it. Pray for the people in your life, and then tell them about Jesus.

DEVOTION

Father, your Son showed us how to pray. He prayed in the morning, he prayed in the evening, he prayed alone, he prayed with others. In hours of distress he retreated into times of prayer. In hours of joy he lifted his heart to you. Help us to pray in this same way and to make prayer a priority in our daily lives.

For more Bible passages on prayer, see Deuteronomy 4:7; Psalm 32:6; Matthew 14:23; 26:36; Luke 6:28; Ephesians 6:18.

To complete the book of John during this twelve-part study, read John 14:15–17:26.

JOURNALING

How can I be more involved in the ministry of prayer?

THE RISEN CHRIST

MAX
LUCADO

REFLECTION

If you only listen to the media news reports, the expression "good news" sounds like an oxymoron. It seems that much of what is called "news" is only the bad, tragic, or shocking stories. This makes it all the more crucial to realize that those of us who know the ultimate "good news" have a wonderful opportunity to bring hope to lost and desperate people. What is the best news you have heard recently? Why was this good news for you?

SITUATION

Each of the Gospel accounts makes one thing very clear: Jesus' followers were not expecting anything to happen on that Resurrection morning. It started out as just another day of grief and confusion. The conclusion of the Sabbath made it possible for some of the women to plan a visit to the tomb, in hopes of doing a better job of wrapping and anointing the body. We don't know how Mary and her companions planned to open the tomb, but they certainly didn't anticipate what they found.

OBSERVATION

Read John 20:1–18 from the NCV or the NKJV.

NCV

¹*Early on the first day of the week, Mary Magdalene went to the tomb while it was still dark. When she saw that the large stone had been moved away from the tomb,* ²*she ran to Simon Peter and the follower whom Jesus loved. Mary said, "They have taken the Lord out of the tomb, and we don't know where they have put him."*

³*So Peter and the other follower started for the tomb.* ⁴*They were both running, but the other follower ran faster than Peter and reached the tomb first.* ⁵*He bent down and looked in and saw the strips of linen cloth lying there, but he did not go in.* ⁶*Then following him, Simon Peter arrived and went into the tomb and saw the strips of linen lying there.*

7He also saw the cloth that had been around Jesus' head, which was folded up and laid in a different place from the strips of linen. 8Then the other follower, who had reached the tomb first, also went in. He saw and believed. 9(They did not yet understand from the Scriptures that Jesus must rise from the dead.)

10Then the followers went back home. 11But Mary stood outside the tomb, crying. As she was crying, she bent down and looked inside the tomb. 12She saw two angels dressed in white, sitting where Jesus' body had been, one at the head and one at the feet.

13They asked her, "Woman, why are you crying?"

She answered, "They have taken away my Lord, and I don't know where they have put him." 14When Mary said this, she turned around and saw Jesus standing there, but she did not know it was Jesus.

15Jesus asked her, "Woman, why are you crying? Whom are you looking for?"

Thinking he was the gardener, she said to him, "Did you take him away, sir? Tell me where you put him, and I will get him."

16Jesus said to her, "Mary." Mary turned toward Jesus and said in the Jewish language, "Rabboni." (This means Teacher.)

17Jesus said to her, "Don't hold on to me, because I have not yet gone up to the Father. But go to my brothers and tell them, 'I am going back to my Father and your Father, to my God and your God.'"

18Mary Magdalene went and said to the followers, "I saw the Lord!" And she told them what Jesus had said to her.

NKJV

1Now on the first day of the week Mary Magdalene went to the tomb early, while it was still dark, and saw that the stone had been taken away from the tomb. 2Then she ran and came to Simon Peter, and to the other disciple, whom Jesus loved, and said to them, "They have taken away the Lord out of the tomb, and we do not know where they have laid Him."

3Peter therefore went out, and the other disciple, and were going to the tomb. 4So they both ran together, and the other disciple outran Peter and came to the tomb first. 5And he, stooping down and looking in, saw the linen cloths lying there; yet he did not go in. 6Then Simon Peter came, following him, and went into the tomb; and he saw the linen cloths lying there, 7and the handkerchief that had been around His head, not lying with the linen cloths, but folded together in a place by itself. 8Then the other disciple, who came to the tomb first, went in also; and he saw and believed. 9For as yet they did not know the Scripture, that He must rise again from the dead. 10Then the disciples went away again to their own homes.

11But Mary stood outside by the tomb weeping, and as she wept she stooped down and looked into the tomb. 12And she saw two angels in white sitting, one at the head and the other at the feet, where the body of Jesus had lain. 13Then they said to her, "Woman, why are you weeping?"

She said to them, "Because they have taken away my Lord, and I do not know where they have laid Him."

14Now when she had said this, she turned around and saw Jesus standing there, and did not know that it was Jesus. 15Jesus said to her, "Woman, why are you weeping? Whom are you seeking?"

She, supposing Him to be the gardener, said to Him, "Sir, if You have carried Him away, tell me where You have laid Him, and I will take Him away."

16Jesus said to her, "Mary!"

She turned and said to Him, "Rabboni!" (which is to say, Teacher).

17Jesus said to her, "Do not cling to Me, for I have not yet ascended to My Father; but go to My brethren and say to them, 'I am ascending to My Father and your Father, and to My God and your God.' "

18Mary Magdalene came and told the disciples that she had seen the Lord, and that He had spoken these things to her.

EXPLORATION

1. At what time of day did Mary visit Jesus' tomb? Why do you think she chose that time?

2. How did Mary react when she saw the stone had been moved from the tomb?

3. How did Mary share the good news she received?

4. Based on her actions, how did Mary feel before and after seeing Jesus?

5. How did Jesus' followers respond to the news that his tomb was empty?

INSPIRATION

The empty tomb never resists honest investigation. A lobotomy is not a prerequisite of discipleship. Following Christ demands faith, but not blind faith. "Come and see," the angel invites. Shall we?

Take a look at the vacated tomb. Did you know the opponents of Christ never challenged its vacancy? No Pharisee or Roman soldier ever led a contingent back to the burial site and declared, "The angel was wrong. The body is here. It was all a rumor."

They would have if they could have. Within weeks disciples occupied every Jerusalem street corner, announcing a risen Christ. What quicker way for the enemies of the church to shut them up than to produce a cold and lifeless body? Display the cadaver, and Christianity is stillborn. But they had no cadaver to display.

This helps explain the Jerusalem revival. When the apostles argued for the empty tomb, the people looked to the Pharisees for a rebuttal. But they had none to give. As A. M. Fairbairn put it long ago, "The silence of the Jews is as eloquent as the speech of the Christians!"

Speaking of the Christians, remember the followers' fear at the crucifixion? They ran. Scared as cats in a dog pound. Peter cursed Christ at the fire. Emmaus-bound disciples bemoaned the death of Christ on the trail. After the crucifixion, "the disciples were meeting behind locked doors because they were afraid of the Jewish leaders" (John 20:19 NLT).

These guys were so chicken we could call the Upper Room a henhouse.

But fast-forward forty days. Bankrupt traitors have become a force of life-changing fury. Peter is preaching in the very precinct where Christ was arrested. Followers of Christ defy the enemies of Christ. Whip them and they'll worship. Lock them up and they'll launch a jailhouse ministry. As bold after the Resurrection as they were cowardly before it.

Explanation:

Greed? They made no money.

Power? They gave all the credit to Christ.

Popularity? Most were killed for their beliefs.

Only one explanation remains—a resurrected Christ and his Holy Spirit. The courage of these men and women was forged in the fire of the empty tomb. The disciples did not dream up a resurrection. The Resurrection fired up the disciples. Have doubts about the empty tomb? Come and see the disciples. (From *Next Door Savior* by Max Lucado)

REACTION

6. Why is Christ's resurrection important for believers? How would Christianity look without the resurrection?

7. Why do you think it is so hard for some people to believe that Jesus rose from the dead?

8. What does Christ's resurrection mean to you?

9. What evidence helps you believe that Jesus rose from the dead?

10. What keeps us from sharing the exciting news of Christ's resurrection with those who don't believe?

11. What objections do people raise about Christ's resurrection? How can we respond to them?

LIFE LESSONS

The personal importance and impact of the resurrection of Jesus is illustrated by the disciples' lives and spelled out in passages like 1 Corinthians 15. The basis of forgiveness takes us back to Christ's death, but the guarantee of all the promises and the hope we live by depends on the truth of the empty tomb. Authentic believers are forever overwhelmed by two conclusions: *Jesus died for me* and *Jesus rose again for me.* In those two statements rests a hope large enough for life and stronger than death.

DEVOTION

Jesus, we thank you for the sweet surprise of Easter morning. We are thankful that when you arose from your sleep of death, you didn't go immediately to heaven, but instead you went and visited people. This visit of love reminds us that people were the reason that you died. We praise your name for that sweet surprise.

For more Bible passages on the Resurrection, see Matthew 22:31–32; John 11:25; Acts 1:22; 4:2, 33; Romans 1:4; 6:5; 1 Peter 1:3; 3:21.

To complete the book of John during this twelve-part study, read John 18:1–20:18.

JOURNALING

How can the victory of Christ's resurrection bring victory to my life?

PETER'S SECOND CHANCE

MAX
LUCADO

REFLECTION

Betrayal, disagreement, misunderstanding, and even exhaustion can fracture a relationship. Firsthand experience in these painful situations often makes us feel that broken relationships are beyond remedy. But God reminds us that what we conclude is impossible, he makes possible every day. Think of a time when you helped to restore a broken relationship. How were you able to help in that situation?

SITUATION

For at least one person, the joy of Jesus' resurrection was overshadowed by shame. Peter remembered his failure. Having boldly proclaimed he would never forsake Jesus, Peter had to eat his words within hours; not once but three times he denied knowing Jesus. Jesus' resurrection suddenly gave him a new perspective. The question that must have lingered in Peter's mind was whether or not Jesus would give him a second chance. Eventually Jesus drew Peter aside for a heart-to-heart talk.

OBSERVATION

Read John 21:1–19 from the NCV or the NKJV.

NCV

¹Later, Jesus showed himself to his followers again—this time at Lake Galilee. This is how he showed himself: ²Some of the followers were together: Simon Peter, Thomas (called Didymus), Nathanael from Cana in Galilee, the two sons of Zebedee, and two other followers. ³Simon Peter said, "I am going out to fish."

The others said, "We will go with you." So they went out and got into the boat. They fished that night but caught nothing.

⁴Early the next morning Jesus stood on the shore, but the followers did not know it was Jesus. ⁵Then he said to them, "Friends, did you catch any fish?"

They answered, "No."

⁶He said, "Throw your net on the right side of the boat, and you will find some." So they did, and they caught so many fish they could not pull the net back into the boat.

⁷The follower whom Jesus loved said to Peter, "It is the Lord!" When Peter heard him say this, he wrapped his coat around himself. (Peter had taken his clothes off.) Then he jumped into the water. ⁸The other followers went to shore in the boat, dragging the net full of fish. They were not very far from shore, only about a hundred yards. ⁹When the followers stepped out of the boat and onto the shore, they saw a fire of hot coals. There were fish on the fire, and there was bread.

¹⁰Then Jesus said, "Bring some of the fish you just caught."

¹¹Simon Peter went into the boat and pulled the net to the shore. It was full of big fish, one hundred fifty-three in all, but even though there were so many, the net did not tear. ¹²Jesus said to them, "Come and eat." None of the followers dared ask him, "Who are you?" because they knew it was the Lord. ¹³Jesus came and took the bread and gave it to them, along with the fish.

¹⁴This was now the third time Jesus showed himself to his followers after he was raised from the dead.

¹⁵When they finished eating, Jesus said to Simon Peter, "Simon son of John do you love me more than these?" He answered, "Yes, Lord, you know that I love you."

Jesus said, "Feed my lambs."

¹⁶Again Jesus said, "Simon son of John do you love me?" He answered, "Yes, Lord, you know that I love you." Jesus said, "Take care of my sheep."

¹⁷A third time he said, "Simon son of John do you love me?" Peter was hurt because Jesus asked him the third time, "Do you love me?" Peter said, "Lord, you know everything; you know that I love you!"

He said to him, "Feed my sheep. ¹⁸I tell you the truth, when you were younger, you tied your own belt and went where you wanted. But when you are old, you will put out your hands and someone else will tie you and take you where you don't want to go." ¹⁹(Jesus said this to show how Peter would die to give glory to God.) Then Jesus said to Peter, "Follow me!"

NKJV

¹After these things Jesus showed Himself again to the disciples at the Sea of Tiberias, and in this way He showed Himself: ²Simon Peter, Thomas called the Twin, Nathanael of Cana in Galilee, the sons of Zebedee, and two others of His disciples were together. ³Simon Peter said to them, "I am going fishing."

They said to him, "We are going with you also." They went out and immediately got into the boat, and that night they caught nothing. ⁴But when the morning had now come, Jesus stood on the shore; yet the disciples did not know that it was Jesus. ⁵Then Jesus said to them, "Children, have you any food?" They answered Him, "No."

⁶And He said to them, "Cast the net on the right side of the boat, and you will find some." So they cast, and now they were not able to draw it in because of the multitude of fish.

⁷Therefore that disciple whom Jesus loved said to Peter, "It is the Lord!" Now when Simon Peter heard that it was the Lord, he put on his outer garment (for he had removed it), and plunged into the sea.

⁸*But the other disciples came in the little boat (for they were not far from land, but about two hundred cubits), dragging the net with fish. ⁹Then, as soon as they had come to land, they saw a fire of coals there, and fish laid on it, and bread. ¹⁰Jesus said to them, "Bring some of the fish which you have just caught."*

¹¹*Simon Peter went up and dragged the net to land, full of large fish, one hundred and fifty-three; and although there were so many, the net was not broken. ¹²Jesus said to them, "Come and eat breakfast." Yet none of the disciples dared ask Him, "Who are You?"—knowing that it was the Lord. ¹³Jesus then came and took the bread and gave it to them, and likewise the fish.*

¹⁴*This is now the third time Jesus showed Himself to His disciples after He was raised from the dead.*

¹⁵*So when they had eaten breakfast, Jesus said to Simon Peter, "Simon, son of Jonah, do you love Me more than these?" He said to Him, "Yes, Lord; You know that I love You." He said to him, "Feed My lambs."*

¹⁶*He said to him again a second time, "Simon, son of Jonah, do you love Me?" He said to Him, "Yes, Lord; You know that I love You." He said to him, "Tend My sheep."*

¹⁷*He said to him the third time, "Simon, son of Jonah, do you love Me?" Peter was grieved because He said to him the third time, "Do you love Me?"*

And he said to Him, "Lord, You know all things; You know that I love You."

Jesus said to him, "Feed My sheep. ¹⁸Most assuredly, I say to you, when you were younger, you girded yourself and walked where you wished; but when you are old, you will stretch out your hands, and another will gird you and carry you where you do not wish." ¹⁹This He spoke, signifying by what death he would glorify God. And when He had spoken this, He said to him, "Follow Me."

EXPLORATION

1. Why did Jesus reveal himself to the disciples in this way? Compare this account with an early encounter between Jesus and the disciples in Luke 5:1–11.

2. How did Jesus restore his relationship with Peter?

3. How did Peter respond to Jesus' words and actions?

4. How did Jesus emphasize the connection between love and service?

INSPIRATION

The sun was in the water before Peter noticed it—a wavy circle of gold on the surface of the sea. A fisherman is usually the first to spot the sun rising over the crest of the hills. It means his night of labor is finally over.

But not for this fisherman. Though the light reflected on the lake, the darkness lingered in Peter's heart. The wind chilled, but he didn't feel it. His friends slept soundly, but he didn't care . . .

His thoughts were far from the Sea of Galilee. His mind was in Jerusalem, reliving an anguished night. As the boat rocked, his memories raced:

the clanking of the Roman guard, the flash of a sword and the duck of a head, a touch for Malchus, a rebuke for Peter, soldiers leading Jesus away.

"What was I thinking?" Peter mumbled to himself as he stared at the bottom of the boat. *Why did I run?*

Peter had run; he had turned his back on his dearest friend and run. We don't know where. Peter may not have known where. He found a hole, a hut, an abandoned shed—he found a place to hide and he hid . . .

So Peter is in the boat, on the lake. Once again he's fished all night. Once again the sea has surrendered nothing.

His thoughts are interrupted by a shout from the shore. "Catch any fish?" Peter and John look up. Probably a villager. "No!" they yell. "Try the other side!" the voice yells back. John looks at Peter. What harm? So out sails the net. Peter wraps the rope around his wrist to wait.

But there is no wait. The rope pulls taut and the net catches. Peter sets his weight against the side of the boat and begins to bring in the net; reaching down, pulling up, reaching down, pulling up. He's so intense with the task, he misses the message.

John doesn't. The moment is deja vu. This has happened before. The long night. The empty net. The call to cast again. Fish flapping on the floor of the boat. Wait a minute. He lifts his eyes to the man on the shore. "It's him," he whispers.

Then louder, "It's Jesus."

Then shouting, "It's the Lord, Peter. It's the Lord!"

Peter turns and looks. Jesus has come. Not Jesus the teacher, but Jesus the death-defeater, Jesus King . . . Jesus the victor over darkness. Jesus the God of heaven and earth is on the shore . . .

Peter plunges into the water, swims to the shore, and stumbles out wet and shivering and stands in front of the friend he betrayed. Jesus has prepared a bed of coals. Both are aware of the last time Peter had stood near a fire. Peter had failed God, but God had come to him.

For one of the few times in his life, Peter is silent. What words would suffice? The moment is too holy for words. God is offering breakfast to the friend who betrayed him. And Peter is once again finding grace at Calvary.

What do you say at a moment like this? What do *you* say at a moment such as this?

It's just you and God. You and God both know what you did. And neither of you is proud of it. What do you do?

You might consider doing what Peter did. Stand in God's presence. Stand in his sight. Stand still and wait. Sometimes that's all a soul can do. Too repentant to speak, but too hopeful to leave—we just stand.

Stand amazed. He has come back.He invites you to try again. This time, with him. (From *He Still Moves Stones* by Max Lucado)

REACTION

5. What hope does this story offer us?

6. How does this story inspire you to handle your mistakes and failures?

7. When have you experienced God's forgiveness in a meaningful way?

8. How can failure destroy a person?

9. What hinders us from accepting and enjoying God's forgiveness?

10. In what failed relationship would you like to experience healing?

LIFE LESSONS

This study began with the promise that these lessons would allow you to discover life as you've never known him before. As you think back over the last few weeks, can you see ways in which God has been bringing about change in your life as you've walked with Jesus? Reflect on the awesome Savior that we follow. Reflect on the personal life lessons you have learned. The Gospel of John closes with hope for Peter and hope for us. There is a future now and forever. God can help us with our failures. Jesus offers us the same quiet, persistent invitation he gave Peter: "Follow me."

DEVOTION

Father, help us as we cope and grapple with yesterday's failures. They weigh us down. Help us to release our regrets to you, Father, and help us to forgive ourselves—even as you have forgiven us—that we might not live burdened and shackled by yesterday's failures, but that we might live free by your grace. Help us follow you, Jesus.

For more Bible passages on forgiveness, see Psalm 130:3–4; Daniel 9:9; Matthew 6:14–15; Acts 10:43; Ephesians 1:7; Colossians 3:13; 1 John 1:9.

To complete the book of John during this twelve-part study, read John 20:19–21:25.

JOURNALING

How can I have the depth of compassion for others that Christ has for me?

Lightning Source UK Ltd.
Milton Keynes UK
UKHW041046190419
341175UK00014B/681/P

9 781418 509446